# *The* Clyde

pocket mountains ltd

Published by
Pocket Mountains Ltd
The Old Church, Annanside, Moffat, DG10 9HB
pocketmountains.com

ISBN: 978-1-907025-35-8

A catalogue record for this book is available
from the British Library

# Introduction

Rivers have been at the centre of Scottish life for thousands of years. For the earliest settlers a river meant survival – a source of food, drinking water and transport. Over the centuries villages, towns and all of Scotland's cities have grown and developed along the banks of a river.

From the Industrial Revolution, when Scotland was one of the manufacturing powerhouses of Europe, until the long decline of heavy industry in the 20th century, rivers were integral to Scotland's economic development.

As towns and cities attempt to reinvent themselves in the wake of that decline, rivers are crucial to regeneration, providing key destinations for residential developments, offices, leisure and recreation. Water activities such as rowing, sailing, kayaking, canyoning, and fishing are increasingly popular, and wildlife is making a comeback as the environment begins to recover from pollution.

From source to sea, a river passes through a variety of landscapes – from mountains to hills, towns to cities, countryside to concrete – and the best way to discover the scenery, wildlife, architecture and history is to walk.

The increasing number of paths and walkways along riverbanks present plenty of opportunities to explore. Whatever your ability – walking at high or low level, following tough terrain or a simple route – this walking guide offers something for everyone.

## The River Clyde

The 25 routes in this book have been chosen to illustrate the varied landscapes, and thus the diversity of walking, to be found on and near the banks of the River Clyde as it travels from source to sea. Many of these routes are circular to take in the best of the scenery in the area around each stage of the river's journey and to explore some of the most interesting towns and villages that have sprung up along its banks. The walks also highlight the wildlife, architecture and history to be found along the way.

For many people, the Clyde still evokes an image of a river dominated by shipbuilding and heavy industry. But choose any of the walks over the Lowther Hills, Culter Fell or the Kilpatrick Hills, follow a route within the woodland of the Clyde Valley or head into the countryside of Upper Clydesdale, and any notion of the River Clyde as an industrial waterway will soon be dispelled.

Select any of the routes around Glasgow, Renfrew, Dumbarton or Hamilton, meanwhile, and you will discover surprising urban beauty.

## In the beginning

Surrounded by the Lowther Hills near the Dumfries and Galloway/South Lanarkshire border, the River Clyde is born at the

confluence of the Potrail and Daer Waters, a little north of the scattering of houses at Watermeetings.

Clydes Burn joins slightly further upstream and it is generally accepted that this modest burn bestows its name upon its bigger cousin. The word Clyde comes from the Cumbric *Clouta*, which loosely translates as 'The Cleansing One'.

The River Clyde is the third longest river in Scotland and the ninth longest in Britain. More than 100 miles long, it stretches through South Lanarkshire, Glasgow, Dumbartonshire, Inverclyde and Argyll & Bute. It runs past the historic market towns of Biggar and Lanark, flows between Hamilton and Motherwell – the former steel capital of Scotland – through Blantyre, past Uddingston, through Rutherglen and Dalmarnock before reaching its upper tidal limit near Glasgow Green. From here it progresses through Glasgow until it widens and deepens at Dumbarton and Port Glasgow, before flowing into the Firth of Clyde at Greenock and Helensburgh.

Throughout its journey, the River Clyde is surrounded by some of southern Scotland's finest scenery. It cascades down waterfalls and snakes through beautiful woodland and fertile agricultural land. An abundance of flora and fauna reside along the entire length of the River Clyde: deer, otter, kestrel, peregrine falcon, skylark, cormorant, butterflies, dragonflies and damselflies,

Erskine Bridge at dawn

wood anemone and greater stitchwort to name only a few.

### Early history

Exploration of the River Clyde and its environs began when hunter-gatherers first followed it in search of food rather than building permanent settlements. There are traces of Neolithic habitation in the area, and in the Iron Age the hills around the Clyde provided an ideal location for building forts, whilst the river also offered a means of getting around.

When the Romans first found their way into Scotland in 80AD, they crossed the River Clyde at Elvanfoot in South Lanarkshire. They went on to build roads, camps and a fort at Crawford.

Along the Clyde another fort was built on Arbory Hill, Tinto Hill was used as a signal station and the remains of Bothwellhaugh Roman Fort and a Roman Bath House can still be seen today in Strathclyde Country Park.

The Romans' greatest legacy in Scotland was the Antonine Wall, which marked the northernmost frontier of the Roman Empire. The western end lies at the base of the Kilpatrick Hills near to Old Kilpatrick, on the banks of the River Clyde.

### The working river

Sea trout and salmon fishing in the Clyde began around the 12th century and it is thought shipbuilding commenced as early as the 15th century.

During the Middle Ages, major settlements such as Dumbarton, Lanark and Glasgow started to flourish. Strategic strongholds such as Bothwell Castle and Craignethan Castle were built during this period, and the river's most famous fort, Dumbarton Castle, dates from the 13th century.

With the arrival of the Industrial Revolution, water as a source of power was key to the location of the mills and factories that sprang up along the Clyde. Mills were established at Biggar, Blantyre and Hyndford, and most famously at New Lanark. Coalmining, engineering and iron- and steel-making also began to prosper.

As trading routes were opened up, Glasgow found itself well positioned due to its location as a port facing the Americas. However, the Clyde was too shallow to accommodate large ocean-going ships, and cargo had to be transferred at Greenock or Port Glasgow. With the rapid expansion of trade in tobacco and sugar, pressure from the merchants – the Tobacco Lords – to deepen the river increased.

During the early 18th century, some of the finest engineers of the time, including John Smeaton, Thomas Telford and John Golborne, devised ways of deepening the Clyde. This project, known as Lang Dyke, ensured that larger ships could navigate the river and dock in the Broomielaw in the centre of the city. Dredging the Clyde continued, which enabled an expansion of international trade.

When shipbuilding replaced trade as the major source of industry, shipyards were established at Govan, Renfrew, Clydebank, Dumbarton, Port Glasgow and Greenock. Yards including Denny's, Fairfield, Yarrow and John Brown were recognised the world over.

More than 25,000 ships have been built on the Clyde, including the *Cutty Sark*, the *Queen Mary*, the *QE2* and *HMY Britannia*. The *Waverley*, the world's last ocean-going paddle steamer, remains on the Clyde today. The term 'Clydebuilt' was synonymous with quality and productivity, and at its peak more than 100,000 people were employed in shipbuilding on the Clyde.

The Great Depression in the 1930s saw the beginning of the irreversible decline of heavy industry along the River Clyde, and there are only a few shipyards operating today. The Stobcross Crane, popularly known as the Finnieston Crane, and the Titan Crane in Clydebank (now a tourist attraction) are landmarks of the industry that shaped much of the Clyde.

### The river today
Glasgow has been forced to reinvent itself as industry and technology have developed, and the Clyde continues to play its part. In recent years established media institutions including the BBC and STV have relocated to the banks of the Clyde, residing alongside popular leisure destinations including the Science Centre, the Riverside Museum and the Scottish Exhibition and Conference Centre.

With the decline of heavy industry the river is now much cleaner. Salmon, grayling and trout are back in abundance. Tourism plays an increasingly important role and trips 'doon the watter' aboard the *Waverley* paddle steamer remain a favourite. It's even possible to take a trip on the seaplane. And then, of course, there's always walking.

Much of the river can be walked using the excellent Clyde Walkway and by walking the 25 routes detailed within this volume you can discover not only the river's incredible industrial heritage, but also the sheer beauty and surprising diversity to be found along its entire 106 miles.

### How to use this guide
The routes in this guidebook run from the Lowther Hills, where the Clyde's journey begins, to the Firth of Clyde where it empties into the sea. Wherever possible, the start/finish for each walk is easily accessible by public transport and, if not, there is car parking nearby. The majority of the walks are also easily reached from the villages and towns along the length of the River Clyde, with access to shops, places to eat, accommodation and public toilets.

Each route begins with an introduction

detailing the terrain walked, the start/finish point (and relevant grid reference), the distance covered, average time to walk the route and the relevant Ordnance Survey (OS) map.

Public transport information is also detailed, although this may change from time to time and should be checked before commencing any of the walks in this guide (travelinescotland.com).

A sketch map shows the main topographical details of the area and the route. The map is intended only to give the reader an idea of the terrain, and should not be followed for navigation – the relevant OS map should always be used for this purpose.

Every route has an estimated round-trip time. This is for rough guidance only and should help in planning, especially when daylight hours are limited. In winter or after heavy rain, extra time should also be added for difficult conditions underfoot.

## Risks and how to avoid them

A few of the routes in this guidebook are challenging hillwalks whilst others cover more remote terrain. The weather in Scotland can change suddenly, reducing visibility to only a few yards. Winter walking brings distinct challenges, particularly the limited daylight hours and the temperature – over higher ground, temperatures can fall well below freezing. Please take this into consideration before commencing any of the hillwalks in this

guide. Preparation for these walks should begin well before you set out, and your choice of route should reflect your fitness, the conditions underfoot and the regional weather forecasts.

Even in summer, warm waterproof clothing is advisable, and comfortable, supportive footwear with good grips is a must. Don't underestimate how much food and water you need and remember to take any medication required, including reserves in case of illness or delay. Do not rely on receiving a mobile phone signal when out walking the hills or in remote areas.

It is a good idea to leave a route description with a friend or relative in case of emergency. If walking as part of a group, make sure your companions are aware of any medical conditions and how to deal with problems that may occur.

There is a route for almost all levels of fitness in this guide, but it is important to know your limitations. Even for an experienced walker, cold, aches and pains can turn an easy walk into an ordeal.

Those routes that venture into the hills or rough terrain assume some knowledge of navigation with map and compass, though these skills are not difficult to learn. Use of Global Positioning System (GPS) is becoming more common; however, while GPS can help pinpoint your location on the map in zero visibility, it cannot tell you where to go next and, like a mobile phone, should not be relied upon.

## Access

Until the Land Reform (Scotland) Act was introduced in 2003, the 'right to roam' in Scotland was a result of continued negotiations between government bodies, interest groups and landowners. In many respects, the Act simply reinforces the strong tradition of public access to the countryside of Scotland for recreational purposes. However, a key difference is that under the Act the right of access depends on whether it is exercised responsibly.

Landowners also have an obligation not to unreasonably prevent or deter those seeking access. The responsibilities of the public and land managers are set out in the Scottish Outdoor Access Code (outdooraccess-scotland.com).

The walks within this guidebook cross land that is only fully accessible due to the co-operation of landowners, local councils and residents. Some of the routes pass through farms, golf courses or streets, and near homes and gardens.

Cyclists and horse riders often use the paths and tracks, and anglers and canoeists may use the river and riverbank. Consideration for others should be taken into account at all times and the Scottish Outdoor Access Code must be followed.

At certain times of year special restrictions are implemented at low level and on the hills, and should be respected. These often concern farming, shooting and forest activities: if you are in any doubt ask. Signs are usually posted at popular access points with details: there should be no presumption of a right of access to all places at all times.

The right of access does not extend to the use of motor vehicles on private or estate roads.

### Seasonal Restrictions

**Red and Sika Deer Stalking:**
Stags: 1 July to 20 October
Hinds: 21 October to 15 February
Deer may also be culled at other times for welfare reasons. The seasons for Fallow and Roe deer (less common) are also longer. Many estates have their own website providing advance notice of shoots.

**Grouse Shooting:**
12 August to 10 December

**Forestry:**
Felling: All Year
Planting: November to May

**Heather Burning:**
September to April

**Lambing:**
March to May – although dogs should be kept on leads at all times near livestock.

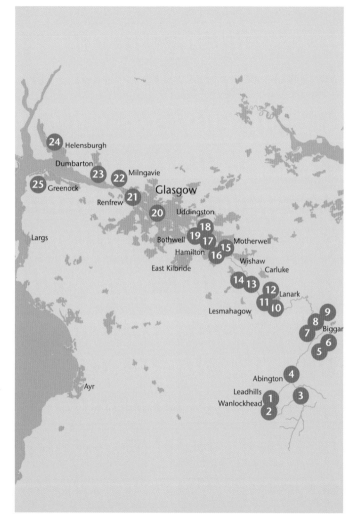

# The Walks

Above Leadhills

The Curfew Bell at Leadhills

# Leadhills and Wanlockhead

**Distance** 6.75km/4.25 miles
**Time** 2 hours
**Start/Finish** Main Street, Leadhills
GR NS887152
**Terrain** Pavement, minor roads, moorland and hill paths and tracks. Short section of pathless terrain where a fence can be followed
**Map** OS Landranger 78
**Public transport** Regular Stuarts Coaches Service 30/31 between Lanark and Leadhills

Although Wanlockhead enjoys the distinction of being Scotland's highest village, neighbouring Leadhills sits an impressive 395m above sea level, making it the second highest. A path running alongside an old railway line provides an easy link with Wanlockhead, with the return journey crossing Wanlock Dod.

▶ From Leadhills Main Street walk south and turn left onto Horner's Place (signposted Leadhills Golf Club). Follow this rough road away from the village to a fork. Go right and walk by the golf course car park and its small wooden clubhouse. After another 50m turn right onto a path beside an old railway line and continue southwest to the signal station of the Leadhills/Wanlockhead Railway Line, which is now a visitor attraction – trains run along the line every weekend between Easter and the end of September.

There's Lead in Them Hills Nestled within the Lowther Hills, Leadhills had a long history as a major centre of lead mining, which began in the 1100s and ended in 1928. During the 1660s, Sir John Hope owned the lead mines, and their subsequent profitability justified building and improving the road network to Leith, more than 50 miles away, so that the ore could be exported.

The most famous Leadhills miner was John Taylor, who reputedly retired aged 117 and died at the remarkable age of 137. Leadhills is also home to the oldest subscription library in Britain, formed in 1741 when 23 miners used their own money to set up the Leadhills Reading Society. Today the library houses the antiquarian book collection, as well as relics of past life in the village and mining records. A collection of minerals unique to the area is also on display.

Other notable residents born in Leadhills include the poet, Allan Ramsay, and William Symington, the builder of the world's first practical steamboat.

Leadhills is also home to the highest golf course in Scotland. At 456m (1500ft) above sea level the views from this challenging course are superb, particularly from the 8th tee.

► Follow the path away from the station where it eventually broadens into a track, passing several old mine relics. It then swings to the right, away from the line, climbing to a path which runs alongside the B797. Pass through a gate beside a cattle grid, then continue towards Wanlockhead.

► Just before entering the village, turn left onto a stony track and accompany this to the Southern Upland Way. Turn right to descend the track back to the B797. Take a left and then second right into Old Library Row (signposted 'Lead Mining Museum').

► Make your way by the museum (see Walk 2 for more information) with the road soon turning right (signposted 'Youth Hostel'). A steep road climb takes you through Wanlockhead by the Miners Library, which was established in 1756. Once by the little row of houses at Goldscaur Row, turn left (opposite Long Row) onto a stony track which sweeps left, then right by a fence onto the lower slopes of Wanlock Dod. An indistinct path climbs north to a line of grouse butts, steering right of these as it rises steeply up Wanlock Dod. After the last butt, the path becomes a little vague, so walk in a northwesterly direction to a fence, turn left onto a wide grassy track and follow this through heathery slopes onto the unassuming summit of Wanlock Dod. This gives fine views of Arran and Tinto Hill, as well as the Lowther Hills.

► The fence turns right here, so cross it and follow the fenceline (which is on your left) to a gate where it splits in two. Don't go through the gate; instead follow a narrow path beside the fence (which is still on your left) as it descends gently northeast towards Leadhills,

**Calling Time** The Scots Mining Company erected The Curfew Bell in 1770 to honour mine manager James Stirling who died that year. Stirling was a renowned mathematician and an astute businessman who joined the Scots Mining Company in 1735. He transformed it from the verge of bankruptcy into one of the most profitable enterprises in Scotland. Just like the principles implemented by Robert Owen at New Lanark, Stirling cut the hours spent underground by the Leadhill miners to a maximum of six per day and improved their working and living conditions, encouraging his employees to build stone cottages and to keep gardens. The Curfew Bell became an integral part of mining life in Leadhills. It informed miners of shift changes and summoned local children to school, as well as warning of mining accidents or people lost in the hills. Today it is used to bring in the New Year.

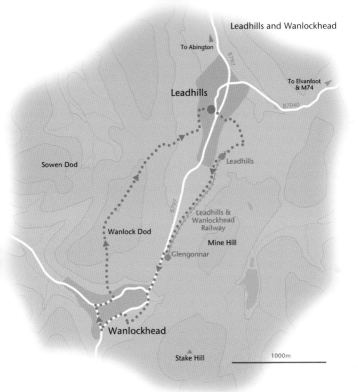

To Abington

B797

To Elvanfoot & M74

B7040

**Leadhills**

Sowen Dod

Leadhills

B797

Leadhills & Wanlockhead Railway

**Mine Hill**

Wanlock Dod

Glengonnar

**Wanlockhead**

Stake Hill

1000m

which lies below. Eventually the path broadens into a track and veers right, away from the fence, to arrive at another track. Turn right onto this and continue down towards Leadhills. As the track swings right, bear left onto an indistinct grassy track.

▶ After about 30m a gate leads into a field. With a fence to your right, descend the field edge towards a radio mast. At the base of the field, continue to follow the fence as it turns left and passes by the mast to a gate. Go through the gate, turn left onto a single-track road, walk by the first house on the left, then turn right and walk down a lane past several houses to reach the Curfew Bell.

▶ Descend by the Curfew Bell into Ramsey Road. Turn right and then left to return to Main Street.

The Museum of Lead Mining in Wanlockhead

Miners' Library at Wanlockhead

# Wanlockhead and the Lowther Hills

**Distance** 11.5km/7 miles
**Time** 3 hours 30
**Start/Finish** Lead Mining Museum, Wanlockhead GR NS873128
**Terrain** Hill paths following section of Southern Upland Way, road
**Map** OS Landranger 78
**Public transport** Regular Stuarts Coaches Service 30/31 between Lanark and Leadhills

**Although Green Lowther – the highest point of the Lowther Hills – rises to 732m (2401ft), this walk begins at Scotland's highest village of Wanlockhead which sits at 466m** (1531ft) above sea level. The route uses road and part of the Southern Upland Way to reach Lowther Hill and Green Lowther. The walking is fairly simple, although it climbs a little up from East Mount Lowther. Marvellous views can be enjoyed from each hill.

▶ Facing the Lead Mining Museum, turn right, follow Old Library Row to the B797 and turn left. Climb the road to reach the wide stony Southern Upland Way track on the right, signposted 'Enterkine Pass to Carronbridge'. The track immediately begins a gradual

**The High Life** Famed as Scotland's highest village, Wanlockhead owes its existence to the silver, gold, copper, lead and minerals that were discovered in the surrounding hillsides. The Romans were probably the first to exploit these deposits and, from the 13th century, groups of miners would journey to the Lowther Hills each summer to work them. Some of the world's purest gold was found here and Wanlockhead became known as 'God's treasure house'.

Wanlockhead was recorded as 'Wenlec' in the mid-16th century, from the Cumbric *Gwynllech*. The Duke of Buccleuch founded a permanent settlement in 1680, when a lead smelting plant and workers' cottages were built, and mining continued here until the 1950s.

Today, visitors can experience going underground into an 18th-century mine at the excellent Museum of Lead Mining. Gold panning taster sessions are available in July and August, and a wonderful collection of rocks, minerals and gold are on display. Explore Wanlockhead Miners' Library, the second oldest subscription Library in Britain, established by miners in 1756 'for our mutual improvement'.

The surrounding Lowther Hills offer plenty of fine walking opportunities and the 212-mile coast to coast Southern Upland Way passes through the village.

ascent past several houses away from Wanlockhead. As it steepens, fine views open out across the village and the large golfball-like structure on top of Lowther Hill looms ahead.

► The gradient then eases as the track travels over open moorland where meadow pipit and grey wagtail enjoy the upland landscape. The track soon drops gently to cross a footbridge where it swings right and continues to rise gradually up the hillside to gain a road. This seems a little incongruous with the surrounding countryside, but is a works road serving the radar and radio masts on the summit of Green Lowther and Lowther Hill.

► Turn right, climb the road and, as it swings sharply left by a metal barrier, turn right onto a narrow path waymarked for the Southern Upland Way (SUW). The path ascends gradually south towards Lowther Hill, crossing the road three times. After the third crossing, turn left and follow a roadside path through a gate to attain the flat summit of Lowther Hill and its radar tracking building. The summit is large enough to avoid the latter – instead enjoy the marvellous views.

► From the summit, rejoin the road (watch out for site traffic) as it descends gently northeast through a gate and then rises gradually by another mast. A steeper drop, then re-ascent leads onto Green Lowther – with far-reaching views over the early stages of the River Clyde to the Daer Reservoir, the Potrail Water, the Culter Hills and Tinto Hill.

► Walk back to the summit of Lowther Hill, turn right and retrace your steps down the outward path. As the works road is reached for a second time, go left and descend to a radio mast. At this point, turn left from the road onto a gravel path. Keeping a fence to your left, the path drops steeply with a stiff climb

Vintage Vantage Point The Lowther Hills form a prominent boundary between South Lanarkshire and Galloway, with Green Lowther and Lowther Hill – the two highest in the range – yielding a fine vantage point of the infant River Clyde as it begins its 106-mile journey. An amble over the Lowther Hills offers the walker an unbroken view that takes in much of Ayrshire, Galloway, South Lanarkshire and the Borders, even extending across the Solway Firth to the mountains of the Lake District. Landmarks seen from Lowther Hill, Green Lowther and East Mount Lowther include the Merrick – the highest hill in Southern Scotland – Criffel on the Galloway Coast and the jagged outline of Arran.

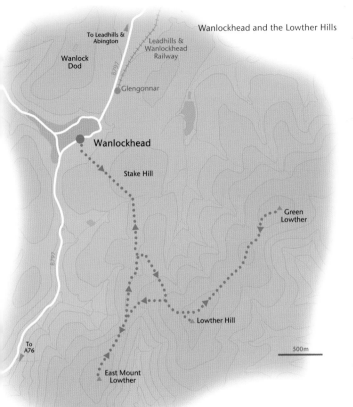

**Wanlock Dod**

To Leadhills & Abington

Leadhills & Wanlockhead Railway

Glengonnar

B797

**Wanlockhead**

**Stake Hill**

**Green Lowther**

**Lowther Hill**

To A76

B797

**East Mount Lowther**

500m

soon proceeding southwest onto the rounded summit of East Mount Lowther. Although lower than its neighbours, East Mount Lowther has a wilder air and makes a good spot to observe the steep hillsides and deep glens so characteristic of the Southern Uplands.

► Retrace your steps down the hillside and, when the path begins to rise, bear left onto a grassy path. This contours north around the hillside, with steep slopes dropping left. Once over a burn the path turns left. It soon becomes a little indistinct, but keep north to return to the outward road. Bear left and walk along the road for around 200m to a SUW sign. Turn left onto the SUW and retrace your steps over the moorland down into Wanlockhead.

Lowther Hill from Green Lowther

# The Potrail and Daer Waters

**Distance** 12.25km/7.5 miles
**Time** 3 hours
**Start/Finish** Watermeetings
GR NS951132
**Terrain** Minor roads, forest and moorland tracks utilising a section of the Southern Upland Way
**Map** OS Landranger 78
**Public transport** Stagecoach Service 102 between Edinburgh and Dumfries will stop on A702 at Watermeetings road end

The scattering of houses at Watermeetings is the starting point for a fine walk that travels alongside both the Potrail and Daer Waters. There are good tracks over some wild and sparsely populated countryside.

► Descend the minor road off the A702, signposted 'Daer Waterworks', cross a bridge over the Potrail Water, then take the rougher track on the right signposted 'Watermeetings'. Follow this track by a farm and cottage, go through a gate, pass by another cottage and then through another gate. Once beyond a third gate, the track enters Watermeetings Forest.

► This track makes easy progress through the landscape, with the Potrail Water below on the right and some superb views of the Lowther Hills. Keep to the main track for around 1.5 miles, heading beneath the wooded slopes of Pin Stane and past a track on the right which leads to Nether Fingland. Beyond this, the track swings left to a fork. Take the right branch to walk along the track as it begins to descend gently around Coom Rig, passing another track on the right. It then veers left by a Southern Upland Way (SUW) signpost, with the SUW joining from the right.

► Now follow the SUW to climb to a crossroads. Go straight on over a stile where the track emerges into a wild, moorland landscape, home to sparrowhawk and kestrel and some remarkable views over the South Lanarkshire countryside. Several stiles are crossed as the walk continues around the lower slopes of Hitterill Hill.

► Carry straight on at a sign for the SUW, passing a track on the right, and remain on the SUW towards Daer Reservoir. The track drops down over a final stile to a junction, where you turn

**Meeting Up** Surrounded by the undulating hills of South Lanarkshire, Watermeetings is the point where the Potrail and the Daer Waters, the two main tributaries of the River Clyde, meet. It is generally accepted that the Clyde got its name from Clydes Burn, which flows into the river just south of Elvanfoot.

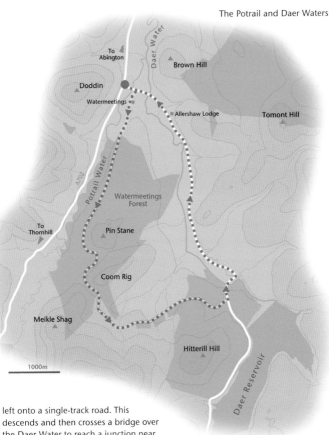

left onto a single-track road. This descends and then crosses a bridge over the Daer Water to reach a junction near the Daer Reservoir.

► Leave the SUW by turning left onto another single-track road, which then undulates gently north through some lovely countryside above the Daer

Water, passing several cottages en route. Once by Allershaw Lodge and Nunnerie Farm, the road crosses back over both the Daer and the Potrail to return to Watermeetings.

27

Above Watermeetings

# Tewsgill Hill and Arbory Hill

**Distance** 12.25km/7.5 miles
**Time** 4 hours 30
**Start/Finish** Lay-by on minor road
west of Crawford GR NS943212
**Terrain** Single-track road, hill and
moorland tracks and paths with
some pathless sections where good
navigational skills would be
required in poorer weather. Several
steep ascents and descents
**Map** OS Landranger 72
**Public transport** Stuarts Coaches
Service 30/31 from Lanark to
Crawford, leaving a short walk to
the start

The hills of South Lanarkshire
provide some fine walking well off
the beaten track. This tough route
over Castle, Raggengill, Arbory and
Tewsgill Hills is a great example,
with striking views that make it
more than worth the effort.

► From the lay-by, facing Castle Hill,
turn left and walk west along the
single-track road to reach a track on
the right. Follow this over fields from
where it veers left and begins a
gradual ascent to reach a radio mast
just beneath the summit of Castle Hill.
This gives fine views north to the
broad flanks of Tinto Hill. A narrow
path then climbs east to the summit
of Castle Hill.

► A featureless section of plateau
drops gently; the route travels northeast
across heathery ground before gaining
height onto the indistinct summit of
Raggengill Hill, which offers a superb
vista to Arbory Hill. Steep, grassy slopes
then descend northeast into a narrow
glen. Here, cross over a broad track and
climb to a wall above a ravine. Follow
the wall (with the wall and ravine to
your left) as it climbs steeply up the
lower slopes of Tewsgill Hill to the head
of the ravine.

► From here turn left, cross the wall
and walk west along an indistinct path

**All Roads lead to Crawford** The Romans left considerable evidence of their travels
in the environs of Tewsgill Hill, including several Roman roads that culminated nearby
at the village of Crawford. In 80AD, the Romans crossed the River Clyde just a little
south at Elvanfoot. Fearing ambush from native tribes, they built a road around Castle
Hill. The extensive views from this point enabled them to spot trouble coming from
some distance.

Situated nearby on the north bank of the Clyde is the ruin of Crawford Castle, which
is believed to date from 1175. During the Wars of Independence it was taken over by
Edward I before being reclaimed by William Wallace and 40 of his men in 1297.

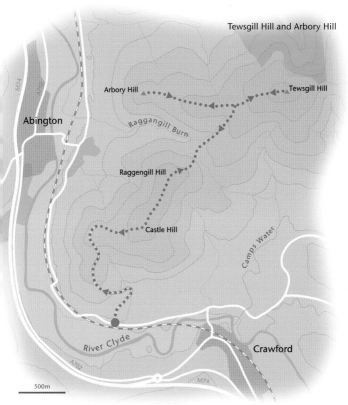

onto Arbory Hill where there are extensive and impressive remains of an Iron Age fort.

► Retrace your steps back to the ravine and then climb east over grassy slopes to the summit of Tewsgill Hill. Just shy of 2000ft, Tewsgill grants an exceptional viewpoint over much of South Lanarkshire and across the Southern Uplands. The simplest return (although this does require one final steep pull) is to descend back to the ravine between Arbory Hill and Tewsgill Hill and follow the wall as it drops into the glen beneath Raggengill Hill. Climb the steep slopes back onto Raggengill Hill, continue over Castle Hill and descend back to the start.

River Clyde from Castle Hill

# Hudderstone and Gathersnow Hill

**Distance** 19.5km/12 miles
**Time** 6 hours
**Start/Finish** Lay-by beside Culter Allers Farm GR NT032313
**Terrain** Single-track road, hill and moorland tracks and paths with some pathless sections where good navigational skills would be required in poorer weather. Several steep ascents and descents
**Map** OS Landranger 72
**Public transport** Stagecoach Service 100 and 102 from Edinburgh to Coulter, leaving a two-mile walk/bike ride to the start

The Culter Water splits the horseshoe of hills above Coulter Reservoir in two. Culter Fell, on the eastern side of the river, is the highest and most popular of the rolling hills of South Lanarkshire. However, the hills to the north and west of the Culter Water are equally worthy of attention. A steep climb over Ward Law leads on to a high moorland plateau offering predominantly good walking conditions, although much of the terrain between Hudderstone and Gathersnow Hill is pathless and, at times, boggy.

► From the lay-by beside Culter Allers Farm (where there is only limited parking), take the left fork and head south along a single-track road which swings left by Birthwood, then carries on alongside the lovely clear Culter Water. The road swings right to cross a cattle grid and here a private road continues – cars cannot be taken any further, but walkers are welcome.

► Walk along the road and, once past a stone sheep enclosure, bear right (opposite a track for Kings Beck) through a gate onto a path. Follow this along a field edge beside the Culter Water to a narrow, wooden footbridge. Carefully cross this, go over a stile, turn left and follow the fence to a gate. Go through the gate and follow a strip of

..........................................................

**A Natural World** The wide-open spaces of Hudderstone and Gathersnow Hill, and the upland plateau between the two summits, provide a diverse natural habitat for a range of wildlife and plant life to prosper. The undisturbed heather moorland is an ideal home for skylark, swift, merlin, hen harrier and buzzard. Crowberry, tormentil, sphagnum moss and common butterwort are all found amongst the blanket bog that occupies the flatter plateau connecting these hills.

woodland (on your right) to its end, then turn right and climb very steeply southwest up the lower grassy slopes of Ward Law. The gradient eases a little as an indistinct path is picked up and bears south onto the rounded 482m summit of Ward Law for a fine view over the flat expanse of the Clyde Valley.

▶ The path continues south as a gradual descent and then re-ascent leads over Woodycleuch Dod. The path broadens into a grassy track which then descends southwest onto a more defined ridge.

▶ This now turns southeast to climb alongside a fence onto Hudderstone. At 626m in height, Hudderstone offers a superb vantage point to survey the surrounding landscape with Tinto Hill's elongated ridge especially eye-catching.

......................................................

The Language of the Hills The origins of the names of the Lowland hills come from languages as diverse as Scots, Anglo-Saxon, Brittonic, Cumbric, Norse and Gaelic. Coomb Dod, Glenwhappen Rig, Dun Law, Glenmuck Height, Culter Cleuch Shank, Turkey Hill, Worm Hill, Snickert Knees, Rob's Bog and Gawky Hill are just some of the intriguing names, which may relate to a person or period in history or describe the shape, colour and height of the hills.

▶ The next stage of the walk to Gathersnow Hill makes its way across a predominantly featureless plateau, which can be boggy in places, so good navigational skills are required in poorer weather.

▶ Descend south from Hudderstone and then southeast along the line of a fence, crossing heathery ground over the flat upland table of Dod Hill, eventually turning east by The Bank to reach a three-way junction of fences. Step over the fence and continue to follow the line of another fence east until a gradual climb leads southeast to a ridge between Hillshaw Head and Gathersnow Hill.

▶ Turn left here and follow another fence and an indistinct path northeast, with steep slopes dropping to the right onto Gathersnow Hill, at 688m the highest point of the walk. There are wonderful views across Coulter Reservoir to Culter Fell and north along the Clyde Valley. Many of the fine Scottish Border Hills like Dollar Law are easily identifiable, as are some of the Galloway Hills.

▶ From Gathersnow Hill, retrace your steps over Dod Hill and back to Hudderstone. A fine descent leads gradually northwest to pick up a great track. Turn right onto this and continue

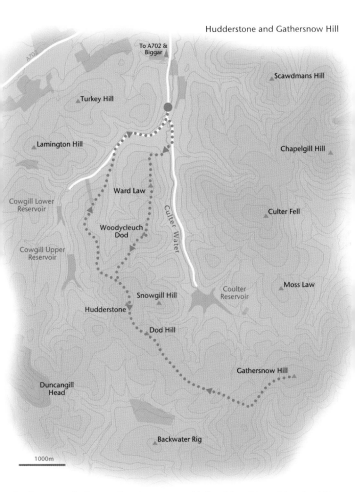

the descent north, then northeast over Cowgill Rig, eventually passing through a gate to reach a minor road. Turn right and follow this quiet road, bearing left by Birthwood Farm to return to Culter Allers Farm.

Chapelgill Hill from Culter Fell

# Culter Fell and Chapelgill Hill

**Distance 16.25km/10 miles**
**Time 5-6 hours**
**Start/Finish Lay-by beside Culter Allers Farm GR NT032313**
**Terrain Single-track road, hill and moorland tracks and paths with some pathless sections where good navigational skills would be required in poorer weather. Several steep ascents and descents**
**Map OS Landranger 72**
**Public transport Stagecoach Service 100 and 102 from Edinburgh to Coulter, leaving a two-mile walk/bike ride to the start**

Sitting just a few metres inside South Lanarkshire on the boundary with the Scottish Borders, Culter Fell is the highest point of the South Lanarkshire Hills. Climbing to 748m, Culter Fell and its satellite peak of Chapelgill Hill (which lies within the Scottish Borders) illustrate the wonderful landscape of Southern Scotland. The rolling aspect of the hills offers infinite possibilities for walking. Culter Fell is a popular hill, and the ascent over Fell Shin travels along a good path, away from the well-trodden route, and over pathless moorland. This walk requires good navigational skills in poor weather.

▶ From the lay-by beside Culter Allers Farm (where there is only limited parking), take the left fork and head south along a single-track road which swings left by Birthwood, then carries on alongside the lovely clear Culter Water. It swings right to cross a cattle grid and here a private road continues – cars cannot be taken any further than this, but walkers are welcome. There are wonderful views along much of the glen with the slopes of Fell Shin and Ward Law particularly prominent.

▶ Continue along the road and, once past a stone sheep enclosure, bear left at a small pinewood onto an obvious track for Kings Beck.

▶ Almost immediately the track forks, so take the right branch onto a faint grassy path which begins to climb steeply southeast over heathery ground. The ascent steepens as the path becomes more obvious, making its way by some grouse butts onto Fell Shin and passing a small cairn. This is a great spot to stop for a breather as the scenery is spectacular, particularly the higher peaks of Woodycleuch Dod and Hudderstone on the western side of the glen and towards Tinto, rising prominently a few miles to the northwest. The gradient eases for a short distance before another fairly steep ascent leads by a second cairn.

It is now a short gentle climb eastwards over boggier ground to reach the summit trig point of Culter Fell.

▶ At the trig point, turn left and descend north, initially quite steeply, following an indistinct path and a line of fenceposts. This leads to a flatter, boggier stretch of ground near to King Bank Head with the path and fenceposts eventually petering out.

▶ From here to Chapelgill Hill the terrain is featureless and good map reading and navigational skills are required in poorer weather. However, in clearer conditions the views are wonderful and, as the route is away from the beaten track, there is a real sense of space with the views extending for miles along the Clyde Valley.

▶ Continue northeast along the more level plateau towards King Bank Head, where some boggier ground has to be negotiated. After a short climb over this hill, an indistinct path is again picked up. Follow this north before bearing right above steeper ground to continue southeast. A gentle descent then leads over a flatter expanse of moorland onto Chapelgill Hill. Once again, fine views await, particularly of Culter Fell and the distant Pentland Hills.

▶ Retrace your steps back to the summit of Culter Fell and then accompany the fenceposts south – which provide a better navigational aid as the path becomes indistinct. A gradual descent towards and over Moss Law again takes you across wetter ground, and a final grassy descent leads down to a track at Holm Nick. Turn right to follow this as it cuts its way through the hilly landscape to reach Coulter Reservoir, a perfect location to catch water from the multitude of burns spilling from the adjacent hills.

Culter or Coulter? Culter/Coulter translates from Scots Gaelic as The Back Land (Cul: back, Tir: land). Both spellings are in use – for example, Coulter Reservoir, Coulter Motte, Coulterhaugh, Culter Waterhead and Culter Allers Farm. Why the spelling difference? Probably nothing more than a mistake that has never been rectified. The flat summit of Culter Fell is the highest point of South Lanarkshire's landscape. Close to Galloway and the Scottish Borders, the views from the trig point at 748m are far-reaching. Gathersnow Hill, Tinto Hill, Broad Law and Drumelzier Law are obvious landmarks but further afield, the long ridgeline of the Pentland Hills, the Merrick (Galloway's highest peak) and the cluster of the Lake District peaks can be identified on a clear day.

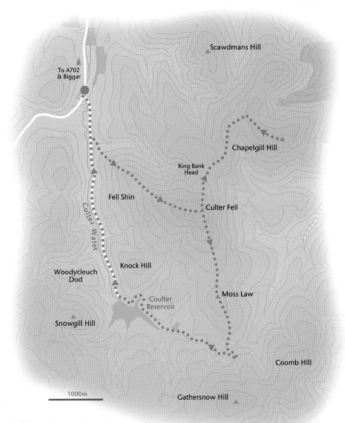

► The track now hugs the shore of the reservoir to reach Culter Waterhead. Here it develops into a road which runs north alongside the Culter Water through a picturesque glen to return to Culter Allers Farm.

Culter Fell from Scaut Hill

Tinto from Fell Shin

# Tinto

**Distance** 11.25km/7 miles
**Time** 4 hours
**Start/Finish** Fallburn car park
GR NS965374
**Terrain** Hill paths and tracks, field edge, roadside verge. Several steep ascents and descents
**Map** OS Landranger 72
**Public transport** Stuarts Coaches Service 191 from Lanark to Fallburn car park road end

Emerging from the predominantly flat lands of the Clyde Valley, Tinto has long been a popular hillwalking destination – the wide track leading from its base to the summit bears testament to this. There are very few days that will not see footfall on Tinto's slopes. Thousands climb to the spacious summit every year to enjoy its 360-degree panorama, and most will descend by the same route. However, a much quieter descent (and scenically just as alluring) is by a good track down over Scaut Hill in the company of skylark, lapwing, kestrel and hen harrier. Returning to Fallburn by this route does, however, require a couple of miles walking along the verge of the busy A73, although most of the walking is away from traffic. The route also crosses farmland, and so dogs should be kept on a lead throughout.

▶ From Fallburn car park, turn left through a gate onto a well-trodden path that progresses through open countryside and rises gently between two fences with Tinto ahead. The gradual climb continues southwest through a gate then beginning to steepen over heathery slopes onto Totherin Hill, home to snipe, wheatear and buzzard.

▶ The track cuts its way around the lower slopes of Totherin Hill, giving the legs and lungs a good workout, and

**Fire and Water** Tinto has been designated a Site of Special Scientific Interest by Scottish Natural Heritage because of its geological significance. There are examples of periglacial stone stripes that have developed over millions of years on Tinto's exposed rocky slopes due to intense freeze/thaw cycles. Tinto's upper slopes are primarily formed from a red-coloured igneous rock known as Felsite, which may explain the derivation of the hill's name – from the Gaelic *Teinnteach*, or 'Fiery Hill'. A more plausible explanation is the actual location of Tinto on what was the main communication route between the Southern Uplands and the Central Belt. It was a beacon hill and a Roman signal station. The summit was also used as a Druidic fire site. The local name for Tinto is Tintock Tap.

then clambers its way over this hill, where a cairn to the left provides a good spot to take a breather and marvel at the extent of the views opening out, particularly the River Clyde tapering its way through the flat plains of the Clyde Valley. The bulky profile of Tinto rises ahead and there is also a good view of Scaut Hill.

▶ In due course the stony track begins a steep ascent, rising away from the deep defile of Maurice's Cleuch (whoever Maurice was has been lost to history; 'cleuch' is the Scots word for gully), with a final steep pull passing a track on the left (to be used on your descent) to reach the vast 711m summit of Tinto. It is adorned by one of the largest Bronze Age burial cairns in Scotland, dating back 3500 years. Birds you may spot near the summit include golden plover and ring ouzel, and there are fine views of the Culter, Pentland and Galloway Hills. On a clear day, Arran and the Lake District are also visible.

▶ From the summit, retrace your steps 100m or so to the track passed on your ascent. Turn right and follow this wide stony track east as it drops gradually down through a gate onto a grassier track. It then continues along a flat, heathery plateau, passing over Scaut Hill where the views continue over Lamington Hill, Hudderstone Hill and the Clyde Valley's patchwork of fields. The track swings round to the right, then left to drop northeast quite steeply towards Wee Hill.

▶ Just before you come to a wall and a small pinewood, bear right onto an indistinct path and follow this down to a burn, which is easily crossed. A more obvious path then climbs over an open field to a conifer wood. Keep to the edge of the wood as you cross Wee Hill to a gate where the path ends. Go through this, now keeping to the field edge as it drops down through a gate into another field. Continue down through a gate to the A73. Cross here, turn left and follow this busier section of road along a verge, passing a small cemetery and St John's Kirk House.

▶ The A72 is then carefully crossed and from here a wider verge follows the A73 back to the entrance road of Fallburn car park. Turn left here and return to the start.

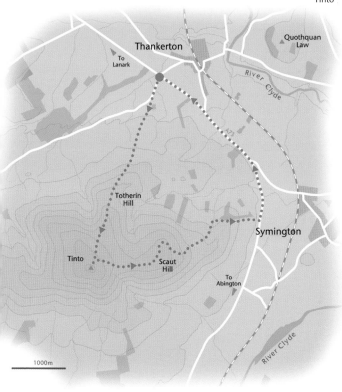

**Is it a Bird?** Tinto is not only popular with walkers but also fellrunners, hang gliders and paragliders. The inaugural Tinto Hill Race took place in 1984 and in the years since it has become a well-established favourite in the hillrunning calendar. Typically, around 200 hardy souls in whatever elements the Scottish weather can throw at them try to run the 4.5-mile route in the quickest time they can. John Brooks of Lochaber Running Club currently holds the record for the fastest time, an incredible 29 mins 58 secs, which he set in 1995.

Summit of Tinto

# Thankerton and Quothquan Law

**Distance** 6km/3.75 miles
**Time** 1 hour 30
**Start/Finish** Corner of Station Road and Sheriffflats Road, Thankerton GR382973
**Terrain** Pavement, single-track road, field-edge and hill. One steep ascent and descent
**Map** OS Landranger 72
**Public transport** Irvine's Coaches Service 191 from Lanark to Thankerton

**The little hill of Quothquan Law, rising above the village of Thankerton, provides one of the finest vantage points along the River Clyde. Much of the Southern Uplands, the rolling hills of the Scottish Borders, and the characteristic agricultural land of the Clyde Valley can be enjoyed from its summit.**

► From the corner of Station Road and Sheriffflats Road, walk south along the pavement through Thankerton, then turn left into Boat Road. Walk across the railway bridge, from which a verge continues to reach a single-track road on the right signposted 'Carnwath, Libberton and Quothquan'. Follow this country road (still Boat Road) to cross the Boat Bridge spanning the broad sweep of the River Clyde – the fields around it are visited by wintering geese during their annual migration.

► Continue by a road on the left, again signposted 'Carnwath, Libberton and Quothquan' and then by Quothquan Law Farm, enjoying great views across the River Clyde towards Tinto Hill and of Quothquan Law's wooded lower slopes, which rise sharply to the left.

► Some 50m beyond the next house turn left from the road, crossing a stile beside a gate into a field. Follow a fence along the right-hand edge of the field, which climbs gradually towards the obvious outline of Quothquan Law to a gate. Go through here and then over a stile into another field. Turn right and climb gently along the field edge to reach a stand of Scots pine. Turn left and follow the edge of the wood beside a fence to another gate.

► Turn right through the gate and here a short but steep climb makes its way up grassy slopes onto the exposed summit of Quothquan Law.

► From the summit, return to Boat Road, turn right and continue back to Thankerton.

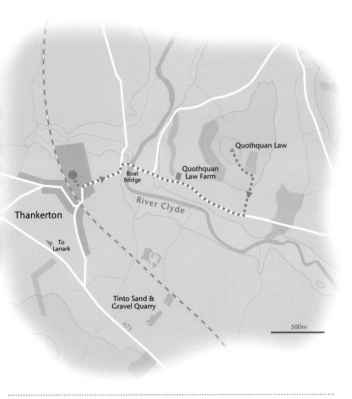

Quothquan Law The curiously named Quothquan Law may be dwarfed by its near neighbour Tinto, but its history is nonetheless interesting. The 335m summit contains the remains of an Iron Age fort which seems to have consisted of two separate enclosures containing a surrounding wall and ramparts. These would have covered most of the summit, providing an easily defensible position and a spectacular viewpoint.

River Clyde from Quothquan Law

Tinto from Biggar

# Around Biggar

**Distance** 5.25km/3.25 miles
**Time** 1 hour 30
**Start/Finish** High Street Biggar
**GR NT043378**
**Terrain** Pavement, single-track road, field paths and tracks
**Map** OS Landranger 72
**Public transport** Stuart's Coaches Service 191 from Lanark to Biggar and Stagecoach Service 102 from Edinburgh to Biggar

**Biggar lies in the heart of some beautiful countryside where the views extend to the higher rolling hills of South Lanarkshire and the Borders. This short but charming walk leaves Biggar's bustling streets to explore the pleasant surroundings of the town.**

► Facing the clocktower at the corner of John Street and High Street, turn right and walk to a pedestrian crossing. Cross High Street into Kirkstyle and follow the pavement as it swings right to climb by Moat Park Heritage Centre. Bear left into Burn Brae Park and descend through the park over a burn via a footbridge.

► Once out of the park a quiet, single-track road leads away from Biggar with beautiful views opening out over the local countryside. After one mile the road turns left, passing by

Hillridge Farm onto a rougher track. Continue to reach a Scottish Rights of Way Society sign ('Springfield 600m, Biggar 2.5km').

► Go straight on through a gate onto a farm track and then through a second gate, where the track continues alongside fields. Where the path peters out, follow the right-hand edge of the field beside a ditch until you come to a gate. Go through this, step over a burn and follow the field, to the left of a ditch, onto a farm track beside another SRWS sign for Springfield and Biggar.

► Turn left to climb to a gate and then onto a minor road at Springfield. Bear left and go down the road, which has superb views towards the Broughton Hills. In due course the road swings right

..................................................

*Biggar's Biggar* The saying, 'London's big, but Biggar's Biggar', alludes to the affection in which the locals hold this attractive market town. The name Biggar derives from the Norse *Bygg gardr*, meaning 'Barley Field', and today Biggar still serves a large rural area. From the 16th century, agriculture and mills were central to the development of the town, which is now perhaps better known for its surprising number and range of museums and heritage centres.

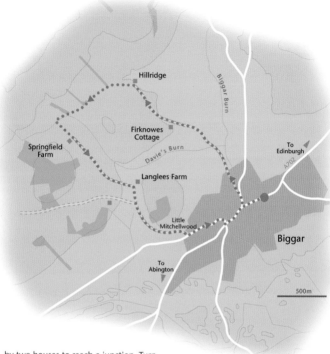

by two houses to reach a junction. Turn left to follow another minor road down towards Biggar.

► As the town draws near, and just before a road junction, bear left through a gate into Little Mitchellwood. At a fork bear right to drop down by the path through a gate. Little Mitchellwood is named after Elizabeth Mitchell, a former owner of the Langless Estate and the first

female town planner in Scotland, who lived near Biggar from 1915 to 1963. During that time she planted the wood that bears her name, which is now looked after by the local community.

► Turn left onto Lindsaylands Road and follow this back down into Biggar at High Street. Turn left and walk back along High Street to the start.

Greater Stitchwort

Sunset near Lanark

# Lanark Loch and New Lanark

**Distance** 6km/3.75 miles
**Time** 1 hour 30
**Start/Finish** Lanark Loch car park
**GR** NS897429
**Terrain** Pleasant parkland and riverbank paths, pavement and single-track roads
**Map** OS Landranger 72
**Public transport** Regular Scotrail Services from Glasgow Central to Lanark

**A thoroughly enjoyable walk begins at the peaceful surroundings of Lanark Loch to visit New Lanark and the historic market town of Lanark, passing some of its most notable buildings on the way.**

► From Lanark Loch car park, descend to the lochside and turn left to follow the track around the quiet waters, enjoying the birdlife. Once you've completed this loop, leave the car park and cross Hyndford Road (A73), turning right to follow the pavement towards Lanark. Cross The Beeches, then turn left and follow a beech-lined track with splendid views over to Tinto. Cross two roads and, after the last beech tree, the track narrows to a path which drops down to meet a road.

► On the opposite side, a woodland path (signposted 'New Lanark') leads down to a road beside a stone bridge. Go straight on, with the road swinging right into New Lanark. Make your way through New Lanark, passing the old Village Store and the Millworkers House, onto New Lanark Road.

► At an old church, bear right and climb a steep flight of steps to reach New Lanark Upper Car Park. Follow the pavement out of the car park, turn right onto Braxfield Road and continue for 0.75 miles into Lanark at Wellgatehead.

► Turn left and descend Wellgatehead to reach the old Tollbooth and the statue of William Wallace. Turn right onto High Street to walk through Lanark's historic centre to a fork. Bear

**Freedom** Translating from Cumbric as 'Forest Glade', Lanark's history dates back to Roman times – a fort was built near the town centre. King Kenneth II held one of the first Scottish Parliaments here in 978. William Wallace, Scotland's greatest patriot and freedom fighter, also lived in the town and it was at Lanark Castle in 1297 that Wallace avenged the death of his wife, Marion Braidfute, when he murdered the English Sheriff, Sir William Heselrig. A statue of Wallace is set into the façade of St Nicholas Church in the High Street. Other notable buildings within the town include the Tolbooth and the Memorial Hall.

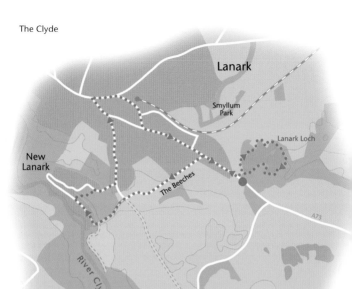

Pass the distinctive octagonal market building (the old auction ring), the magnificent St Mary's Church and the old Cartland Bridge Toll Gates, dating from 1820, to return to the car park at Lanark Loch.

right into Bannatyne Street and carry on to a roundabout. Cross the entrance of a retail park back onto Hyndford Road.

**Those Magnificent Men in their Flying Machines** *The Spirit of Flight*, the eye-catching sculpture which stands at the entrance to Lanark Loch, commemorates the 1910 Air Show in Lanark, the first airshow in Scotland and the second British International Airshow. Between the 6th and 13th of August, 250,000 spectators watched 17 aviators from seven countries demonstrate their flying skills. The three tonne sculpture stands 6.5m tall and features replicas of three of the historic aircraft – the Bristol Box Kite, the Bleriot and the Antoinette – which flew at the show more than 100 years ago.

Aviation sculpture at Lanark Loch

Lanark Loch

# New Lanark and the Falls of Clyde

**Distance** 11.25km/7.5 miles
**Time** 3 hours
**Start/Finish** Upper car park, New Lanark GR NS882427
**Terrain** Easy woodland and riverbank paths with some steep ascents, pavement and single-track roads
**Map** OS Landranger 72
**Public transport** Regular Scotrail Services from Glasgow Central to Lanark. Stuarts Coaches Service 135 from Lanark to New Lanark

New Lanark's status as a UNESCO World Heritage Site is down to the legacy of David Dale and his son-in-law, Robert Owen. In the 19th century, their pioneering socialist ideals provided the workers at New Lanark's cotton mills – particularly women and children – with proper working and welfare conditions. Many of the original buildings are open to the public, and a visit can be combined with a walk along the River Clyde to the spectacular Falls of Clyde. Peregrine falcon and red squirrels may also be seen on this route. During autumn the colours radiating from the beech and birch trees are exquisite, whilst in spring wildflowers such as bluebell and wild garlic provide a riot of colour and smell.

▶ From the upper car park, descend the steep path to New Lanark Road, turn left and walk along the pavement past the visitor centre to a fork. Take the left track to a flight of steps, ascending these to go through a stone doorway. Bear

**The New Lanark Co-op** David Dale was already a successful businessman when he built the cotton mills at New Lanark in 1777. He was born the son of a grocer in the Ayrshire town of Stewarton in 1739 and, having served a weaving apprenticeship in Paisley, he set up a yarn-importing business in 1763. In 1799 Dale's daughter Caroline married Robert Owen, who subsequently bought the New Lanark mills from Dale for £60,000 in 1800. Robert Owen was born in the small market town of Newtown in Wales in 1771, and his driving ambition throughout his life was to improve the health, education and rights of the working class. Along with his father-in-law, Owen was one of the founders of the cooperative and socialist movements of the early 19th centuries. During his 25 successful years running New Lanark, Owen created a model community where children under ten were not allowed to work in the mills, free medical care was provided, as was a comprehensive education system for both children and adults.

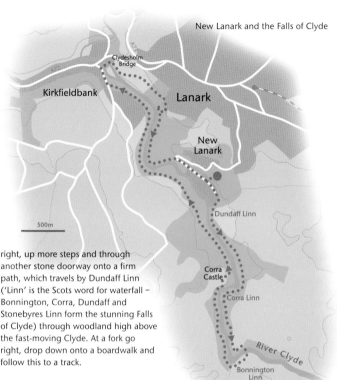

right, up more steps and through another stone doorway onto a firm path, which travels by Dundaff Linn ('Linn' is the Scots word for waterfall – Bonnington, Corra, Dundaff and Stonebyres Linn form the stunning Falls of Clyde) through woodland high above the fast-moving Clyde. At a fork go right, drop down onto a boardwalk and follow this to a track.

▶ Turn right onto the track, which becomes a single-track road, and pass a cottage and then Bonnington Linn Power Station. At this point turn right onto a path which carries on to a flight of steps. These make the steep climb high above the Clyde to a viewpoint and a spectacular panorama of the gorge and the magnificent 28m-high Corra Linn (this scene was painted by the celebrated British landscape artist J M W Turner in 1802).

▶ From the viewpoint turn left, then right up more steps, passing a signpost for Bonnington Linn. The woodland path meanders above the gorge, passing the peregrine falcon hide, with superb views along the Clyde. Once down another flight of steps, continue to a fork. Bear left and follow the path to a weir.

► Turn right, cross the weir, then turn right onto a path and follow this past the dramatic Bonnington Linn to reach a fork. Turn right, cross a footbridge and walk along the high-level path which hugs the line of the cliffs and undulates through the woodland, eventually passing the remains of Corra Castle.

► From Corra Castle the path drops sharply past Corra Linn and travels along the banks of the river, in due course crossing a footbridge to then climb to a fork. Take the right branch, signposted for Kirkfieldbank, and follow this above Dundaff Linn with New Lanark across the river. The path then swings left away from the Clyde to meet a track. Turn right to follow the track into woodland and continue as it crosses a stone bridge above a dramatic waterfall to eventually bring you out at Kirkfieldbank.

► Turn right, going down Kirkfield Road, then turn right onto Riverside Road at a signpost for the Clyde Walkway. Cross the Clyde by the old Clydesholm Bridge and then turn right through a gate beside a row of cottages. Descend the single-track road to a gate. Go through here onto a grassy track and, beyond another gate, a path climbs steeply, swinging right onto St Patrick's Road.

► Follow this quiet road to a Clyde Walkway sign. Turn right into Castlebank Park and continue to another Clyde Walkway sign. Turn right and drop steeply down steps which zigzag through woodland to the River Clyde.

► The path then crosses a footbridge and carries on alongside the river before climbing steeply up more steps. Once over another footbridge, the path zigzags gradually uphill back to New Lanark Road. Turn right and follow the pavement back into New Lanark.

**Going Batty** Perched on a cliff edge overlooking the Clyde, the 15th-century Corra Castle was perfectly positioned for defensive purposes. It is said that Mary Queen of Scots slept at Corra Castle after the Battle of Langside but, like most accounts of Mary's whereabouts at certain points in her life, the story remains unsubstantiated. At the bottom of the gorge there used to be a cornmill and a dungeon, which is now home to daubenton's, natterer's and whiskered bats. It is thought the castle is used as a maternity roost for the bats between March and October.

Corra Linn

Above New Lanark

Golden Saxifrage, Cleghorn Glen

Red Campion, Mouse Water

Lesser Celandine, Cleghorn Glen

Wood Sorrel, Cleghorn Glen

David Dale House at New Lanark

# Lanark and the Mouse Water

Distance **8km/5 miles**
Time **2 hours**
Start/Finish **Lanark Railway Station
GR NS886436**
Terrain **Parkland, woodland and
riverbank paths, pavement and
single-track roads**
Map **OS Landranger 72**
Public transport **Regular Scotrail
services from Glasgow Central
to Lanark**

**Cartland Crags National Nature
Reserve, which sits above the Mouse
Water, a tributary of the River Clyde,
is a segment of the woodland that
cloaks much of the Clyde Valley and
is home to a variety of animal and
plant life. The reserve is one of the
highlights of a lovely walk that sets
out from the busy streets of Lanark to
drop through the woodland to
Kirkfieldbank. From here, parkland
and wooded paths climb to the
outskirts of New Lanark to then return
by pavement to Lanark.**

▶ From Lanark Railway Station turn
right onto Bannatyne Road and walk
down over South Vennel into High
Street. Follow the busy pavement
through the town, keeping right of
St Nicholas Church with its imposing
William Wallace statue, crossing Hope
Street and North Vennel and then
turning right onto Mousebank Road.

Walk along this quiet street, crossing
several side streets onto a quiet country
road which drops gradually by a school
and then a cottage before swinging left
to cross the Mouse Water. Once over the
bridge, continue for a few metres and
then turn left over a wooden footbridge
into Cleghorn Glen, part of the Cartland
Crags National Nature Reserve.

**Wooded Wonderland** Cartland Crags
and Cleghorn Glen are just two of the
eleven woods that form the Clyde Valley
Woodlands Special Area of
Conservation. The dramatic gorge that
cuts through the reserve was formed
after the last ice age when meltwaters
from glaciers scoured through the
bedrock. The reserve has outstanding
examples of the ancient, semi-natural
and deciduous woodland that would
have once covered great swathes of
lowland Central Scotland. The mix of
acidic and limestone soils within the
woodland create the right conditions for
ash, elm, sycamore, hazel, alder, oak,
birch and Scots pine to dominate,
together with occasional stands of
aspen. Within the reserve, particularly
during the spring and summer months,
common varieties of wildflower such as
bluebell, red campion, wild garlic, lesser
celandine, and primrose thrive, whilst
rarer plants, including golden saxifrage,
wood fescue, and yellow star of
Bethlehem, can also be found.

► Follow the woodland path as it climbs steeply above the Mouse Water. The gradient quickly eases and makes for a thoroughly enjoyable walk high above the gorge. In due course, you cross a wooden footbridge, after which the trail becomes a red gravel path. This makes a gradual ascent, granting fine countryside views. Another three footbridges are crossed in quick succession with this well-maintained path continuing its gentle ascent.

► A fairly steep descent begins to drop in between two fences and then down a flight of wooden steps to reach the impressive Cartland Bridge at the A73. Don't cross the bridge; instead carefully cross the A73 onto a road signposted 'Nemphlar'. The road immediately forks – take the left branch into Sunnyside Road. Walk along the minor road as it swings left onto Mousemill Road, which then crosses a lovely stone bridge over

the Mouse Water. The road passes by Clyde Valley Caravan Park to meet the A72 at Kirkfieldbank.

► Cross the A72, turn right and then walk over Kirkfieldbank Bridge, with the River Clyde flowing underneath and a great view of Clydesholm Bridge. Turn left onto Riverside Road (at a Clyde Walkway sign) and follow it round to go back over the Clyde by the Clydesholm Bridge. Once across, turn right through a gate beside a row of cottages. Descend the single-track road to a gate. Go through here onto a grassy track where, beyond another gate, a path rises steeply and swings right onto St Patrick's Road.

► Follow this quiet road to a Clyde Walkway sign. Turn right into Castlebank Park and continue to another Clyde Walkway sign. Turn right and drop steeply down steps which zigzag

**Clyde Crossings** There are many wonderful bridges spanning the River Clyde and its tributaries. One such example is the Cartland Bridge, its three imposing arches straddling the Mouse Water. The great engineer, Thomas Telford – best known for the Caledonian Canal and the Menai Bridge – designed it in 1822. Unfortunately, for much of the year, the Cartland Bridge is hidden from view by tall trees, but glimpses of it can be spotted en route to Kirkfieldbank. There are also two bridges spanning the River Clyde at Kirkfieldbank. The modern bridge which carries the A72 was built in 1959, but the adjacent and far more charismatic Clydesholm Bridge was constructed between 1694 and 1699, making it the oldest crossing of the Clyde. Prior to 1959 the Clydesholm Bridge carried traffic across the river, but it is now a footbridge and part of the Clyde Walkway.

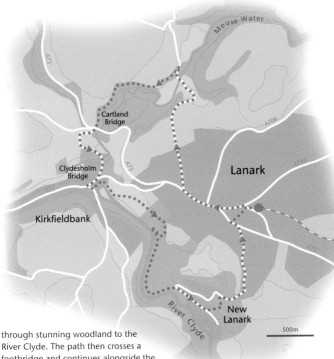

through stunning woodland to the River Clyde. The path then crosses a footbridge and continues alongside the river before climbing steeply up more steps. Once over another footbridge, the path zigzags gradually uphill back to New Lanark Road.

▶ Turn right and follow the pavement towards New Lanark, but before reaching the village turn left at an old church and climb a flight of steps taking you high above New Lanark. At the top turn right, follow the pavement out of the New Lanark upper car park and then turn right onto Braxfield Road. Follow Braxfield Road into Lanark at Wellgatehead. Bear left, then turn right into South Vennel and follow the pavement as it climbs gently to Bannatyne Street. Turn right to return to the railway station.

Clydesholm Bridge

Bluebell Wood, Nethan Gorge

# Crossford and Craignethan Castle

**Distance** 6.5km/4 miles
**Time** 1 hour 30
**Start/Finish** Corner of Braidwood Road (B7056) and Lanark Road (A72) GR NS827464
**Terrain** Pavement, single-track road, woodland paths
**Map** OS Landranger 72
**Public transport** Regular Stuarts Coaches Service 317 from Hamilton to Crossford

The village of Crossford sits at the heart of the beautiful Clyde Valley, which is best known for the orchards and garden centres that are strung out along much of its length. Sitting above Crossford are the historic remains of Craignethan Castle. A beautiful woodland path rises steeply from Crossford above the River Nethan and through the Nethan Gorge – which is alive with animal and plant life, particularly during the spring and summer months – to reach Craignethan Castle. Some quiet roads with exceptional views across South Lanarkshire pass through Tillietudlem before returning to Crossford.

▶ From Braidwood Road (B7056), cross Lanark Road (A72), turn right and walk through the village of Crossford, which sits on the banks of the Clyde. Continue by the Tillietudlem Inn and over Blair Road (which leads to Craignethan Castle if driving). Once over the River Nethan, immediately turn left from Lanark Road into Nethan Gorge.

▶ Follow a good path, though it can be boggy in parts, through this peaceful slice of woodland as it begins to rise gradually above the River Nethan. It soon starts to climb steeply up two flights of steps leading high above the gorge and the river.

▶ The path then drops down over a footbridge and climbs a third flight of steps where the gradient now eases and the path hugs the edge of the gorge.

Just Gorge-ous The Clyde Valley Woodlands National Nature Reserve includes Nethan Gorge, and there is historic evidence that the woodland surrounding the gorge has been managed since the Middle Ages, its uses including timber for buildings and livestock pasture. Today the gorge is dissected by one of the River Clyde's tributaries, the River Nethan, and comprises the Upper and Lower Nethan Gorges. The Lower Nethan, in particular, presents one of the finest examples of semi-natural woodland surviving within the Clyde Valley. Ash, oak, and elm play host to song thrush, willow warbler and yellowhammer, while the ground cover includes wood sorrel and bluebells.

There are fine views through the trees over the South Lanarkshire countryside and across the gorge towards Craignethan Castle.

► At a fork beside the corner of a conifer plantation, go left and continue above Nethan Gorge with the path eventually dropping steeply down a flight of steps to reach the base of the gorge. A footbridge takes you over the River Nethan. At a fork, turn left up more steps to meet a gate. Go through this gate to reach a road beside the impressive walls of Craignethan Castle. Turn right and make your way to the entrance of this fascinating castle. Under the care of Historic Scotland, it is open every day between April and September and at weekends only between October and March.

► From the castle entrance, climb the road and walk through the car park onto a single-track road. Follow this through delightful open countryside with great views across South Lanarkshire to reach a gate at the hamlet of Tillietudlem. Turn left onto Corra Mill Road, which descends gently by a scattering of houses with further fine views, particularly to the little hill fort above Hazelbank. This quiet road drops more steeply, crossing the River Nethan by a bridge, and then zigzags uphill by Corra Mill through peaceful countryside, the gradient easing at the junction with Blair Road.

**Craignethan Chronicles** Craignethan Castle is located above the River Nethan and is still in remarkably good condition. It was designed by the nobleman and architect Sir James Hamilton of Finnart, the illegitimate son of James Hamilton, the 1st Earl of Arran. Work began on Craignethan Castle in 1532, three years after the death of Sir James' father, and was completed in 1536. During this time Sir James had become one of the richest landowners in Scotland and also held the position of King James V's Master of Works. He was responsible for the restoration of Linlithgow Palace and Blackness Castle, and created the Renaissance palace at Stirling. Despite his wealth and position, Sir James made powerful enemies and King James accused him of treason. Although this was not proven, he was executed in 1540. Craignethan Castle did not survive the turbulent conflict of the Reformation – although it did shelter Mary Queen of Scots prior to her defeat at Langside in 1568 – and was slighted in 1579. The remains illustrate how impressive the building must have been in its heyday. It is widely thought that Craignethan Castle was the inspiration for Tillietudlem Castle in Sir Walter Scott's novel *Old Mortality*. The nearby hamlet adopted the name of Tillietudlem after publication of the book.

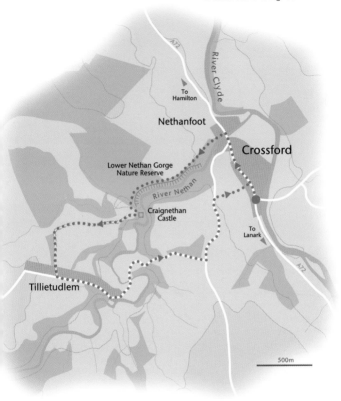

To Hamilton

River Clyde

Nethanfoot

Crossford

Lower Nethan Gorge
Nature Reserve

River Nethan

Craignethan Castle

To Lanark

A72

Tillietudlem

500m

▶ Turn left onto Blair Road and follow this by a few houses. As the route drops down towards Crossford, it gives exceptional views over the village and the River Clyde, as well as southeast along the Clyde Valley towards Tinto. On the approach to Crossford, turn right onto a hedge-lined path signposted 'Lanark Road'. This excellent little path drops gently down to reach Lanark Road (A72) opposite Crossford Parish Church. Turn right and continue through Crossford back to Braidwood Road.

Craignethan Castle

Above Crossford and the Clyde

Wood Anemone, Milton Lockhart

# Crossford and General Roy

**Distance** 9.5km/6 miles
**Time** 2 hours 30
**Start/Finish** Corner of Braidwood
Road (B7056) and Lanark Road (A72)
GR NS827464
**Terrain** Pavement, riverbank and
woodland paths, single-track road
**Map** OS Landranger 72
**Public transport** Regular Stuarts
Coaches Service 317 from Hamilton
and Lanark to Crossford

Where would we be without Major-
General William Roy? Lost probably.
His name may not be instantly
recognisable, but his contribution to
the maps we use to navigate our way
around our towns, cities, hills,
mountains and countryside is
indisputable. His ingenuity in using
new scientific discoveries led to the
mapping of the entire British Isles.
Roy was born at Milton Head, near
Crossford in 1726, and a monument
dedicated to him stands by the
roadside at his birthplace. A
picturesque section of the Clyde
Walkway, where kingfisher, heron,
otter and goosander may be spotted,
leaves from Crossford into Milton
Lockhart Woods. Once by Milton
Head, quiet country roads with
some excellent views across the
surrounding countryside lead back
to the Clyde Walkway and a simple
return to Crossford.

▶ From the corner of Lanark Road and
Braidwood Road, walk along Braidwood
Road and over the elegant Crossford
Bridge which spans the River Clyde.
Once by the Valley International Park
entrance, turn left off the road through a
gate with information board onto the
Clyde Walkway. Follow the path down to
the Clyde where it turns right.

**The Apple Store** There is a long
tradition of fruit-growing in the Clyde
Valley dating back to the early
monasteries and medieval times. The
fertile lands and a sheltered landscape,
particularly the flat pastureland between
Crossford and Maudslie, provided the
ideal climate for growing fruit. By the
end of the 18th century, it is estimated
that more than 60 varieties of apples
and 24 of pears were grown in the Clyde
Valley. By the late 19th century, villages
such as Hazelbank, Kirkfieldbank and
Crossford flourished as a result of fruit
cultivation, and the area became known
as Scotland's 'Garden of Eden'.

In the 1920s fruit production went
into decline as a result of increased
competition from global markets,
although by the 1950s the Clyde Valley
had become synonymous with tomato
production. Today, there are local efforts
to regenerate neglected orchards and
revive fruit cultivation in the Clyde Valley
to meet the growing demand for local,
high-quality food produce.

▶ A well-maintained path accompanies the banks of the River Clyde away from Crossford, crossing a bridge over a burn and then passing through a gate. Carry on through a second gate, from where the peaceful path now makes its way over a boardwalk, up a flight of steps and then down more steps to a fork. Take the left branch for a lovely stretch of path which hugs the banks of the Clyde, surrounded by open countryside.

▶ Keep an eye out for kingfisher and heron as you progress along the path, crossing another bridge before passing through a series of gates to eventually cross an open field. Once through another gate, the path forks. Take the left branch over a bridge onto a boardwalk, which leads to a steep flight of steps. The path then veers left and climbs up more steps, taking you high above the Clyde. Stick to the path as it rounds a narrow gorge leading to another flight of steps which drop steeply back down to the Clyde. Beyond another bridge, a glorious section of the Clyde Walkway continues along the riverside, over a final footbridge and through another gate onto an open field. Walk along the field-edge path to a gate.

▶ Turn right through the gate at a Clyde Walkway sign and climb steps into Milton Lockhart Woods, a Site of Special Scientific Interest. The path, lined with wildflowers such as ramson, greater stitchwort and wood sorrel, meanders through ash, elm and beech trees and up a flight of steps to a narrow road. Turn right and follow this as it rises gently away from the Clyde Walkway to a fork. Go left and walk along this quiet country road to reach Miltonhead and the monument to military engineer and surveyor William Roy who was born nearby in 1726.

**Map Quest** Following the Jacobite Rebellion of 1745, the Hanoverian military commanders in Scotland commissioned a map of the Scottish Highlands recording roads, settlements, bridges, forests, hills, mountains and fields. William Roy was one of the men given the responsibility of mapping the country. Using a number of innovative techniques, he worked on the survey between 1747 and 1755, and the hand-drawn map he produced became known simply as 'The Great Map'. It was the precursor to the Ordnance Survey maps we rely on today. Roy's vision extended to the establishment of an organisation responsible for mapping and surveying in Britain. In 1791, a year after Roy's death, this would become known as the Ordnance Survey. Appropriately, the memorial to General Roy at the site of his birthplace near Carluke is a trig point pillar.

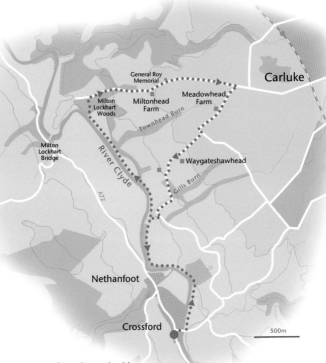

Milton Lockhart Bridge

River Clyde

A72

Milton Lockhart Woods

Milton Lockhart

General Roy Memorial

Miltonhead Farm

Meadowhead Farm

Townhead Burn

Gills Burn

Waygateshawhead

Carluke

Nethanfoot

Crossford

500m

► Continue along the road, with pleasant views towards Carluke, for around half a mile to a junction. Turn right and follow another quiet road, which swings sharply to the left by Meadowhead Farm. After a short distance, turn right onto a narrow road with views towards Motherwell and Hamilton. It descends by some cottages, Waygateshawhead House and Farm and the remains of an old tower.

► The road then drops down over a bridge, turns right by Wicketshawgill Farm and then left to reach a track signposted for the Clyde Walkway on the right. Leave the road and walk along the track to a gate beside the outward path. Turn left onto the Clyde Walkway and retrace your footsteps back to Crossford.

Fisherman at Crossford

# Dalzell Estate and Baron's Haugh

**Distance** 5.5km/3.5 miles
**Time** 1 hour 30
**Start/Finish** Dalzell Estate car park
GR NS755553
**Terrain** Lochside and parkland paths
and tracks
**Map** OS Landranger 64
**Public transport** Regular Scotrail
trains from Glasgow Central to
Airbles, leaving a short walk to start

The River Clyde hits urbanisation at
Motherwell and Hamilton on its
journey towards Glasgow. Despite
the built-up nature of this
environment, there are sanctuaries
with a wonderful variety of wildlife.
One such refuge is Baron's Haugh
Nature Reserve on the outskirts of
Hamilton. Excellent paths make their
way around the reserve and the
historic Dalzell Estate.

► Walk through the RSPB car park to
pick up a path, which skirts woodland
as it descends towards the loch. At a
junction turn right onto a solid path
and, after passing a path on the left
leading to a bird hide, turn left at the
next path and follow this through rowan
and beech woodland to reach a paved
track. Turn left out of the wood and
walk along the track beside the River
Clyde, where kingfisher and heron may
be spotted. The track continues, passing
more hides, for around a mile to meet a
gate. Go straight on through the gate
and follow the trail beside the Clyde to
another gate.

► Go through here into woodland. The
route rises steeply away from the Clyde
to gain a broader track. Turn left and
climb steadily to a fork. Go left
(signposted 'Dalzell House') to progress

**Hamilton's Haven** Originally a Royal Hunting Forest, this land was developed as an
estate by the Dalzell Family of Lanarkshire in the 13th century. In 1647, it was
granted to James Hamilton 1st of Dalzell, and was passed down through successive
generations until 1952. Over the centuries, extensive additions were made to the
grounds and to Dalzell House. Archibald Hamilton (1694-1774) was a keen
horticulturist who created a wealth of paths and walks around the estate, many of
which still exist. Baron's Haugh – *haugh* is an old Scots word for a 'low-lying
meadow beside a river' – was part of the estate and provided summer grazing for
livestock; now cattle are a feature of the landscape once again. Baron's Haugh was
purchased by the RSPB in 1983, and provides a habitat for a variety of birdlife,
including whooper swans, goldeneye, nuthatch, redshank and ringed plover.

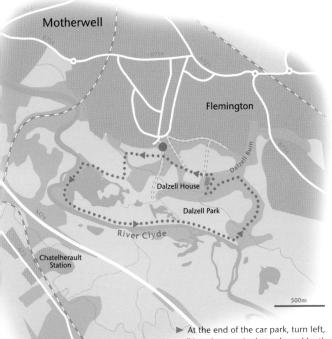

Motherwell

Flemington

Dalzell Burn

Dalzell House

Dalzell Park

River Clyde

Chatelherault Station

500m

through fine woodland to meet a path on the right. Descend this path to a fork, go left, continue above a steep-sided gorge and then drop down some steps. Once over a bridge, climb more steps, then turn left and follow a woodland track through Dalzell Estate and go around a barrier into a car park.

▶ At the end of the car park, turn left, walking down a single-track road by the impressive Dalzell House to reach the Japanese Garden, which was created in 1920 and modelled on a traditional Japanese garden. Turn right to make your way through the garden, cross over a narrow bridge and climb a flight of steps. Continue to a woodland path, turning left to follow this over a single-track road to a fork. Take the right branch and carry on over a single-track road back to the car park.

Damselfly at Baron's Haugh

Cadzow Oak

# Chatelherault and the Avon Gorge

Distance **7.5km/4.5 miles**
Time **2 hours**
Start/Finish **Chatelherault car park
GR NS737540**
Terrain **Easily navigable woodland
and riverbank paths with some
gradual climbs**
Map **OS Landranger 64**
Public transport **Regular Scotrail trains
from Glasgow Central to Chatelherault**

This lovely circular route leaves from
Chatelherault, one of Scotland's most
historic and beautiful buildings, to
follow firm waymarked paths and
tracks. It travels through woodland
and above the spectacular Avon
Gorge where beech, oak and birch
trees play host to kingfishers,
stonechat, squirrels, roe deer and
otter. You may also spot a rare breed
of white cattle, supposedly bred by
the Dukes of Hamilton from the
ancient 'wild kye' of Scotland. The
walk also visits the magnificent
Cadzow Oaks, some of which date
back as far as the 12th century.

▶ Facing the main entrance of the
visitor centre, walk left to descend a
path and turn left onto a woodland
path, signposted 'Green Bridge Route'.
Make your way along the path through
mixed woodland, passing a car park on
the left. The path runs alongside a golf
course and a line of Scots pine before
meandering its way through peaceful
beech woodland high above the Avon
Gorge. Where the trees thin, open
countryside presides with great views
south over Lanarkshire towards Tinto.

▶ Eventually the track drops gently to a
fork. The right branch leads down to the
White Bridge (it is a short diversion of
around 0.5km down several flights of
steps deep into the gorge to reach this
bridge spanning the Avon Water); for
the Green Bridge, however, take the left
fork. The track continues to travel
through woodland, the path lined with
wildflowers in the spring and summer,
and there are views towards the nearby
town of Larkhall. In due course, the
track begins to zigzag its way steeply

**16th-century Town Twinning** The name Chatelherault originates from the French
town of Châtellerault. The title Duc de Châtellerault was presented to James
Hamilton, 2nd Earl of Arran, in 1548, and to subsequent Dukes of Hamilton.
Formerly the estate grounds, Chatelherault Country Park surrounded the magnificent
Hamilton Palace which was demolished in 1921 due to subsidence. In 1734, the
renowned architect William Adam built Chatelherault Hunting Lodge to provide
estate buildings, stables and kennels for James Hamilton, 5th Duke of Hamilton.
Adam is said to have jokingly called the lodge, 'the dog kennels of Hamilton'.

down several flights of steps (careful, some may be slippy), then levels out and continues to reach the Green Bridge spanning the Avon Water.

► From the bridge, there are fine views along the river. Once across, rejoin the woodland path and follow this as it climbs rapidly, taking you high above the gorge. Stick to the main path, passing the Millheugh Steps, and continue to reach a fork.

► Take the right branch (the left option leads to the small village of Quarter), continuing along the path to eventually cross a lovely old stone bridge. The track then swings right and carries on until it reaches a signpost.

► Ignore the path on the right; instead walk straight on along the path signposted for the Cadzow Oaks. Follow this until it drops steeply down into the secluded Divoty Glen. There are a fantastic variety of wildflowers here throughout spring, whilst during autumn the beech woodland leaves provide a kaleidoscope of stunning colours. The path crosses a stone bridge and then sweeps right to climb away from Divoty Glen. Once over another bridge, the path soon swings right to reach the Cadzow Oaks, their great, thick girths and gnarled trunks and branches an impressive sight.

► Turn left from the main track and make your way by the oaks along a grassy path to rejoin the main track. Turn left, descend over a bridge and continue along the track to reach a fork. Bear right and drop down past the remains of Cadzow Castle, which was built in 1530, though there has been a castle here since the 12th century – originally as an occasional royal residence of King David I.

► The Duke's Bridge is then crossed; this magnificent structure, high above the Avon Water, offers some spectacular views along the river. Once across this, a single-track road leads you on a gradual ascent to a fork. Turn right and follow the road a short distance back to the visitor centre.

**Avon Calling** The Avon Water begins its 24-mile journey in the hills of Distinkhorn and Wedder Hill above Kilmarnock in East Ayrshire, and joins the River Clyde near Hamilton. The name Avon is derived from the Gaelic *Abhainn* and simply means 'River'. From Ayrshire, the Avon Water makes its way through South Lanarkshire and into the magnificent Avon Gorge, the river having cut a dramatic cleft through Chatelherault Country Park.

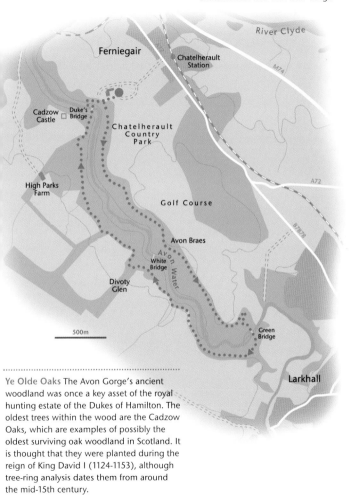

**Ye Olde Oaks** The Avon Gorge's ancient woodland was once a key asset of the royal hunting estate of the Dukes of Hamilton. The oldest trees within the wood are the Cadzow Oaks, which are examples of possibly the oldest surviving oak woodland in Scotland. It is thought that they were planted during the reign of King David I (1124-1153), although tree-ring analysis dates them from around the mid-15th century.

The Hunting Lodge at Chatelherault

Hamilton Mausoleum

# Hamilton and Low Parks

Distance **5.25km/3.25 miles**
Time **1 hour 30**
Start/Finish **Low Parks car park
GR NS724562**
Terrain **Pavement, single-track road,
woodland paths**
Map **OS Landranger 64**
Public transport **Regular Scotrail
trains from Glasgow Central to
Hamilton**

**A short walk through the streets of
historic Hamilton visits some of the
finest buildings outside of Scotland's
main cities. Built on the banks of the
River Clyde, Hamilton has a rich
history and there is much to learn on
this fascinating walk.**

▶ From the car park beside Strathclyde
Park Golf Course, turn left onto Mote
Hill and follow the pavement down to
reach the splendid Hamilton
Mausoleum where time would be
well spent walking its perimeter and
admiring the exceptional stonework
and design.

▶ Retrace your steps along Mote Hill,
which sweeps left to a junction. Cross
Mote Hill, turn left and continue by Low
Parks Museum which, as the oldest
building in Hamilton, is very much
worth a visit – it is also home to the
Cameronian Museum.

▶ Bear right onto Muir Street. Cross the
road and follow it up to reach the
elaborate Watson Fountain. John
Watson was the 1st Baronet of Earnock
(an ancient estate in Hamilton) and one
of Scotland's leading coalmasters
during the 19th century. Continue past
Montrose Crescent then turn left into

**What's in a Name** Hamilton was originally known as Cadzow, or Cadyou, and the
name still appears around the town on buildings and street names. During the Wars
of Scottish Independence, Walter fitz Gilbert, who was the head of the Hamilton
family and governor of Bothwell Castle, initially sided with the English. After the
Battle of Bannockburn, however, he gave his support to Robert the Bruce. For this, he
was granted estates along the Clyde Valley, including Cadzow. It was renamed
Hamilton by James Hamilton, 1st Lord of Hamilton.

When James Hamilton married Princess Mary Stewart – sister of King James III – in
the 1470s, the Hamilton family advanced to the highest echelons of Scottish nobility.
With the arrival of the railway in the 19th century, Hamilton grew rapidly and
became a major industrial town – coal mining and iron smelting transformed its
economy and surrounding landscape. Today, Hamilton is the fifth largest town in
Scotland with a population of around 50,000.

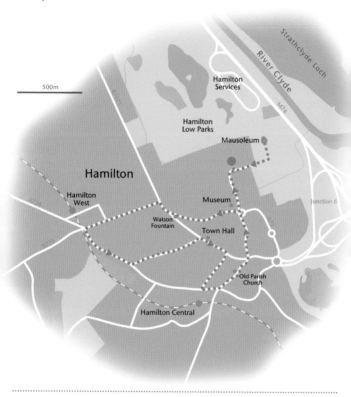

**A Fitting Finale** Hamilton Mausoleum is one of the finest buildings in Central Scotland. This outstanding example of Roman-styled architecture was completed in 1858, a full 16 years after work began. It was built to be a more fitting resting place for the Dukes of Hamilton – prior to this the family burial vault stood nearby in the old, dilapidated Collegiate Church. The 123-ft high facade reputedly holds the longest-lasting echo of any man-made structure in the world. The coffins of the Duke of Hamilton and his ancestors were later re-buried in Bent Cemetery, due to the subsidence and flooding that affected the mausoleum.

Almada Street. Pass the impressive Sheriff Court building to reach Union Street. Turn left to go down Union Street, passing some fine stone villas, to Auchingramont Road.

▶ Turn left and walk along Auchingramont Road, again passing beautiful stone residences, to reach Cadzow Street and Hamilton Town Hall, one of the finest buildings outside of Scotland's cities. The impressive St Mary's Church sits a short distance to the left.

▶ Turn right, walk down Cadzow Street past the town hall and over a roadbridge with great views of the mausoleum, and then swing right into Leechlee Road, passing Hamilton Old Parish Church. Completed in 1734, this fine Georgian church, with its striking clocktower, is the only church ever built by renowned architect William Adam.

▶ Leechlee Road continues to Brandon Street. Turn left onto the pedestrianised Quarry Street, which leads back to Cadzow Street.

▶ Go straight on into Castle Street, pass the town square and over Muir Street onto Mote Hill. Retrace your steps to the car park.

**Worth the wait** Such was the scale of the magnificent Hamilton Town Hall that it was built in stages. Andrew Carnegie, the great industrialist and philanthropist, opened the library section in 1907; King George V opened the townhouse offices in 1914, and the town hall was completed in 1928. In 2002, Hamilton Town Hall underwent a major refurbishment: £9 million was spent restoring both the interior and the A-Listed exterior of this splendid building.

Hamilton Town Hall

Roman Bath House

# Strathclyde Loch and the Roman Bath House

**Distance 6km/3.5 miles**
**Time 1 hour 30**
**Start/Finish Bothwellhaugh car park**
**GR NS723583**
**Terrain Lochside paths and tracks**
**Map OS Landranger 64**
**Public transport Regular Scotrail**
**trains from Glasgow Central to**
**Airbles, leaving a short walk to start**

Following a simple circuit, a walk around Strathclyde Loch provides an easy couple of hours in which to enjoy fine views, a variety of wildlife and some intriguing history. Strathclyde Park has a lot of lovely quiet little corners, whilst the loch conceals the lost village of Bothwellhaugh. The walk also visits the historic Roman Bath House, dating from around 142AD. The site of a Roman Fort is nearby.

▶ From the Bothwellhaugh car park, walk towards the loch and the main country park road. Turn left, follow the pavement over the entrance road to a hotel, then cross the main road onto a path. Go left at a fork and follow the path down to the loch. Turn left and walk along the solid path beside the loch, which teems with birdlife such as cormorants, swans, geese, gulls and a variety of ducks.

▶ As you approach an old pavilion, the path veers left away from the loch to pass the pavilion and a car park. Continue through a pocket of woodland and then turn left from the main path to

**The Lost Palace** Situated amidst the urban sprawl of Motherwell and Hamilton, Strathclyde Park is located on the site of what used to be known as the Low Parks of Hamilton Palace. Hamilton Palace was the former seat of the Dukes of Hamilton and one of the grandest houses in Scotland when it was built in 1695.

It was demolished in 1921, due to subsidence caused by the excavation of coal from nearby Hamilton Palace Colliery. Bothwellhaugh was the name given to a low-lying expanse of pasture near the village of Bothwell and during the 1880s it became the site of one of the largest mining villages along the Clyde Valley. The colliery, known locally as 'the Pailis', employed more than 1400 workers when producing at its peak. Sadly, when it closed in 1959, Bothwellhaugh rapidly declined and the last houses were demolished in 1966. In the 1970s, the artificial creation of Strathclyde Loch meant flooding the last derelict remains of Bothwellhaugh, consigning the village to the past. The loch is now the centrepiece of Strathclyde Country Park.

accompany another path towards the main road. Upon reaching a junction, take the second path on the right, which leads over a footbridge, then turn right and follow the path down to the well-preserved remains of the Roman Bath House.

► The Bath House was unearthed in the 1970s and later rebuilt above its original position to allow it to be viewed by the public. Originally, it would have comprised a sequence of bathing rooms, including one housing a hot plunge bath, two warm rooms and the furnace and changing rooms, as well as an ice cold pool for an invigorating plunge. The latter is a challenge now enjoyed in the loch itself as it has in the past hosted the annual Great Scottish Swim event, as well as being the official triathlon venue for the 2014 Commonwealth Games.

► Continue by the Bath House back towards the loch, passing through some fine woodland, a habitat for a variety of thrushes and chats. In due course the path swings left away from the loch to a fork. Take the right branch and continue through more woodland back to the loch. It is then a simple matter of following the path to the loch's southeastern end.

► The path then swings right to run alongside the main country park road, passing a weir, with the River Clyde to your left, to reach the entrance

**Roman Retreat** Until 139AD, the demarcation line of Roman-occupied Britain was Hadrian's Wall. When Antoninus Pius became emperor, however, he ordered the army further north to build a second wall along a new frontier between the Forth and Clyde estuaries. Forts were built along the length of what became known as the Antonine Wall as well as at other strategic points south of it to ensure the safe passage of troops and supplies to the front line. Although only faint traces remain, it is thought that the fort at Bothwellhaugh could have supported a garrison of around 500 men.

The Roman Army realised that cleanliness reduced the chances of infection and ill health, consequently improving the efficiency of the soldiers, and so a visit to the bathhouse was part of their regular routine. It would have resembled something akin to a present-day Turkish Bath, with soldiers cleaning themselves by sweating the dirt from their skin. Heat was provided by a furnace at one end of the building, and the hot air it produced passed underneath the floor of three heated rooms and up through the wall cavities. The bathhouse was first excavated in 1975/6.

of the Strathclyde Park Watersports Centre, where you can see boats and yachts sailing on the loch. Rowing events held here include the 1986 Commonwealth Games. Walk through the car park by the sailing club and Scottish Rowing Centre and then back onto a lochside path. Follow this past another car park to a broader track, which doubles as a cycle track. Turn right onto this and carry on along the

loch shore to its northwestern extremity. Here, the track swings left to reach a road.

▶ Go straight across this onto a path, which travels around the head of the loch through woodland to a fork. Bear left to a crossroads, bear left again and continue to the main road. Cross the road and turn left to reach the start at Bothwellhaugh car park.

111

Cormorants on Strathclyde Loch

Bothwell Bridge

# Bothwell Castle and the David Livingstone Centre

**Distance** 5.5km/3.5 miles
**Time** 1 hour 30
**Start/Finish** Bothwell Castle car park
GR NS689594
**Terrain** Pavement, single-track road,
woodland paths
**Map** OS Landranger 64
**Public transport** First Glasgow Service
255 from Glasgow to Bothwell

The 13th-century remains of
Bothwell Castle are the starting
point for a walk that is as historically
interesting as it is varied. Taking
advantage of superbly maintained
paths, the route follows the wooded
banks of the River Clyde to reach the
David Livingstone Centre, which
celebrates the life of Scotland's
greatest explorer and missionary.
From here, it is onto pavement
through the attractive leafy streets
of Bothwell to reach Bothwell
Bridge, the scene of one of the
country's most famous battles.

▶ From the car park walk through a
gate and onto a track. Turn right and
follow this anticlockwise around
Bothwell Castle to reach another gate.
Go through this onto the Clyde
Walkway, which travels along the banks
of the River Clyde through beech, oak
and sycamore woodland. After crossing

a small stone bridge, follow the path to
reach a fork. Take the left branch and
this takes you on a gradual ascent to
another fork. Go right here and follow
the path back down to the Clyde. On
gaining another path, go left and carry
on along the riverbank with the David
Livingstone Centre coming into view.

▶ The path then climbs to a gate. Turn
right through this, then immediately
right again to cross the impressive David

*Castle on the Clyde* The striking red
sandstone façade of Bothwell Castle has
an enthralling history. In 1242, Walter of
Moray, whose ancestry lay in Scotland's
North East coast, acquired the lands of
Bothwell. Work quickly began on the
castle, and money was lavished on its
design, particularly the magnificent
circular keep that still stands today. The
castle passed between Scots and English
hands no fewer than six times during
the Wars of Independence. During the
14th century, the 'Black' Douglas family
(through the marriage of Joanna Moray
and Archibald the Grim) acquired the
Castle, and over the next 25 years a new
towerhouse, a great hall and a chapel
were added. Throughout subsequent
centuries, Bothwell Castle had many
different owners until it was placed in
the care of Historic Scotland in 1935.

Livingstone Memorial Bridge, which spans the River Clyde and was opened in 1999. The first footbridge between Blantyre and Bothwell was built in 1852 to replace a ferry service that plied its trade 200m upstream from here. Once over the bridge, turn left onto Station Road and follow this a short way to the David Livingstone Centre, which is well worth a visit (open Mar-Dec).

► Retrace your steps over the bridge but go straight on, passing the outward path, and accompany a narrow road on a gradual climb towards Bothwell, joining a pavement at Blantyre Mill Road. Follow this, passing Clyde Terrace, and turn right onto Mill Road.

► Walk along the pavement, turning left onto St Andrews Avenue and then continue to Hamilton Road (B7071).

Walk briefly down this road before bearing right onto Old Bothwell Road. This drops steeply to Bothwell Bridge back at Hamilton Road.

► From Bothwell Bridge, follow the pavement northwest along Hamilton Road as it climbs gently back into Bothwell. Stop and admire the many red sandstone buildings along the way, particularly the magnificent Bothwell Parish Church, home to an elaborate monument to Joanna Baillie, a renowned poet and dramatist who was born in Bothwell in 1762. Continue through the town by the Bothwell Bridge Hotel and then, at a sign for Bothwell Castle, turn left onto Blantyre Road, then right onto Castle Avenue. Walk along the pavement for around a mile to reach the entrance drive. Turn left and follow the road back to the castle at the start.

**Dr Livingstone I Presume** From humble beginnings, David Livingstone became renowned as a missionary and an explorer of Africa. He was born in 1813 in the mill village of Blantyre, just a stone's throw from the David Livingstone Centre, a National Trust for Scotland property that celebrates his life and achievements. Working at the local mill from the age of 10, Livingstone educated himself, studied theology in Glasgow and was ordained as a minister in 1840. He first visited Africa in 1841 as a missionary, fervently opposing the slave trade. He returned to Africa several times, with his final trip in 1866 a failed attempt to find the source of the River Nile. Livingstone subsequently lost contact with the rest of the world for six years, and Henry Stanley was commissioned to find him. When he did, it is said he greeted him with the now famous words, 'Dr Livingstone, I presume?' Livingstone was determined not to leave Africa until his mission was complete. He died of malaria and dysentery in present-day Zambia in 1873.

**The Battle of Bothwell Brig** In 1679, following the Restoration of King Charles II, Covenanters opposed to the Government enjoyed a minor victory at the Battle of Drumclog (near Strathaven). A force of around 4000 Covenanters, nominally led by Sir Robert Hamilton, then set off to take Glasgow but met 5000 of the Duke of Monmouth's dragoons and militia near Hamilton at Bothwell Bridge instead.

On 22 June 1679, the battle began and, although the Covenanters put up stiff resistance for two hours, they were disorganised and overwhelmed. Taking revenge for the defeat at Drumclog, John Graham of Claverhouse gave no quarter and as many as 600 men were killed in the rout. Many hundreds more were taken to Edinburgh, imprisoned in Greyfriars Kirkyard, and later transported to the colonies. A memorial to the Covenanters was erected beside Bothwell Bridge in 1903.

Bothwell Castle

Pacific Quay sunrise

# Kelvingrove and Glasgow Green

**Distance** 14km/8.5 miles
**Time** 3 hours 30
**Start/Finish** Kelvingrove Art Galleries
GR NS567664
**Terrain** Riverside walkway,
pavement, park paths
**Map** OS Landranger 64
**Public transport** Regular buses and
trains from across Scotland to
Glasgow. The Glasgow Underground
stops at Kelvingrove

**Much of Glasgow's history can be
observed through its distinct and
much loved architecture, which
ranges from the outstanding
Kelvingrove Art Gallery to the
landmark Finnieston Crane. Many of
these wonderful buildings are
visited on a route that travels along
Glasgow's historic streets and
through two of its finest parks.**

► Facing Kelvingrove Art Gallery, turn
right to walk along Argyll Street onto
Sauchiehall Street. Turn right onto
Radnor Street and cross Argyll Street
onto Haugh Road, before turning left
onto Yorkhill Street then right onto
Kelvinhaugh Street. Continue to reach
Sandyford Street, and turn left to walk
underneath an old railway bridge.
Immediately turn right and cross a
footbridge over the Clydeside
Expressway (A814) to drop down
onto Stobcross Road.

► Bear right at the roundabout to pass
the Scottish Ambulance Service Heliport
on Stobcross Road, turning right here to
access the Clyde Walkway. Turn left by
the River Clyde where, looking back,
you'll see the masts of one of the last
remaining Clyde-built tall ships berthed
at the Riverside Museum, Scotland's
Museum of Transport and Travel.

► The path veers left by the Clyde
Auditorium, known locally as the
Armadillo, and Finnieston Crane onto
Lancefield Quay (A814). Carry on across
Finnieston Street and past the Clyde Arc
bridge to continue along Lancefield Quay.
Follow the Clyde Walkway as it continues

**Artistic Masterpiece** First opened in
1901, Kelvingrove Art Gallery and
Museum is one of the finest buildings in
Glasgow. The story of Kelvingrove being
built back-to-front by mistake, and the
subsequent suicide of its architect, has
entered urban mythology. The intention
always was to build it with the grand
entrance facing Kelvingrove Park. For
many years the museum displayed some
of the world's finest art, including
Salvador Dali's mesmerising *Christ of St
John on the Cross* and paintings by the
Glasgow Boys. However, it wasn't until a
multi-million pound refurbishment in
2006 that 8000 exhibits – almost double
what the museum held previously –
could be displayed.

underneath the Kingston Bridge to reach the triangular Tradeston Bridge.

► Cross the bridge, then turn left to walk along Clyde Place. Go under the railway lines which cross the George V Bridge to reach Carlton Place.

► Cobbled streets take you by some splendid Georgian architecture; turn left onto South Portland Street Bridge. Once across, turn right onto Clyde Street and follow this past Victoria Bridge before crossing Crown Street to enter Glasgow Green through the McLellan Archway, leaving the busy city streets behind.

**Clydebuilt** Shipbuilding on the River Clyde peaked immediately prior to the First World War, when it was estimated that 100,000 people in Glasgow were directly or indirectly employed by the industry. Yards including Fairfield, Yarrow, and John Brown built famous ships such as *HMS Wild Goose*, *HMS Indomitable* and the *QE2*. However, during the Great Depression of the 1930s, around 60% of shipbuilding workers were made redundant and by the 1960s the industry was in irreversible decline. There are still a few specialist shipyards in operation although new industries such as financial services provide more employment along the banks of the Clyde today.

► Walk straight through the park past the towering Nelson Monument towards the People's Palace. Turn left through a gate and walk around the People's Palace to reach the Doulton Fountain.

► Leaving the fountain, turn left back into Glasgow Green and continue through the park, exiting by the McLellan Archway. Turn right onto the Saltmarket and follow the pavement over London Road and Gallowgate onto High Street at Trongate – one of the oldest streets in Glasgow – passing the magnificent Tolbooth Clock. High Street climbs steadily all the way to Cathedral

**Dear Green Place** Glasgow has more than 90 parks within its boundaries, and the oldest is Glasgow Green. It was given to the people of Glasgow in 1450 by King James II and used as common grazing ground and a place to wash and bleach linen. The first of the city's 'steamies', or communal washhouses, opened here in 1732.

Over the years, the Green has played host to political meetings, anti-war demonstrations and rock concerts. Landmarks include the Doulton Fountain, which was gifted to Glasgow as part of the International Exhibition of 1888 and moved to the Green in 1890. After restoration work in 2004, the fountain was placed in a new location in front of the People's Palace, a museum dedicated to the history of Glasgow first opened in 1898.

Square, home to Glasgow Cathedral and Provand's Lordship, Glasgow's oldest house.

► Turn left onto Cathedral Street and continue by Queen Street Railway Station, crossing Buchanan Street onto Bath Street. Continue to Hope Street, and turn right and then left onto Sauchiehall Street for a gradual climb.

► At Rose Street, turn right and then left into Renfrew Street to pass the renowned Glasgow School of Art, which was built in 1897 by the celebrated architect Charles Rennie McIntosh. Renfrew Street descends to a footbridge which crosses St George's Road onto Woodside Crescent.

► Follow the pavement round to Claremont Terrace, with Trinity Tower up to your right. Go straight on into Kelvingrove Park (passing the Granite Steps), immediately forking left and descending through the park to the River Kelvin. Turn right, following the river, and then cross it via the Prince of Wales Bridge. Bear left out of Kelvingrove, cross over Kelvin Way and back into the park to follow the path before re-crossing the Kelvin to return to the start on Argyll Street.

Doulton Fountain, Glasgow Green

Kelvingrove Art Gallery and Museum

The Renfrew Ferry

Renfrew Town Hall

# Renfrew, the Clyde and the Cart

**Distance** 6km/4 miles
**Time** 1 hour 30
**Start/Finish** War Memorial, Hairst Street GR NS506676
**Terrain** Pavement, single-track road, woodland paths
**Map** OS Landranger 64
**Public transport** McGills Buses Service 23 from Glasgow to Renfrew

Renfrew is located at the confluence of the River Clyde and the White Cart Water. This is reflected in the Cumbric translation of Renfrew, which means 'Point of the Current'. The town of Renfrew, sitting a little to the west of Glasgow, is an ancient Royal Burgh with a fascinating history. This pleasant walk travels along the banks of both rivers, passing some fine buildings and visiting locations of historical significance.

► From the War Memorial on Hairst Street, follow the pavement down by the Town Hall, passing High Street onto Canal Street. Walk by the Brown Institute and bear left onto Ferry Road, continuing to Meadowside Street. Cross straight over this street and continue down Ferry Road to reach the River Clyde and the slipway for the historic Renfrew/Yoker Ferry.

► Make your way back to Meadowside Street, crossing at the traffic lights and then turning right to follow this street over a bridge to a road on the left. Follow this a short distance, then turn right through a barrier onto a solid tarmac path signposted 'Inchinnan Road via the River Clyde'. The path makes its way past an industrial site and a strip of woodland, passing some large old red-brick buildings, before eventually bearing right to reach the River Clyde.

**Royal Renfrew** In 1315, Walter Stewart, Baron of Renfrew (the current Baron is Prince Charles), married Marjory, daughter of Robert the Bruce. Their son, Robert II of Scotland was born in 1316 and was the founder of the House of Stewart. Since then, Renfrew has been hailed as the 'Cradle of the Royal Stewarts'.

The Clyde has played a central role in Renfrew's growth and as far back as the 16th century the residents of the town had exclusive rights to fish for salmon on the river. By the end of the 19th century, Renfrew was home to a number of shipyards, employing many of the townspeople at a time when shipyards on the Clyde produced a third of all ships built worldwide. Today Renfrew has settled into the commuter belt servicing Paisley and Glasgow. The town is dominated by the magnificent 160ft-high Town Hall, opened in 1877, replacing the old Tolbooth, which was first built in 1670.

► The path swings left and follows the course of the river where fantastic views of the Kilpatrick Hills, Erskine Bridge and the famous Titan Crane preside, granting a good sense of the Clyde's industrial past. Continue past the green navigation beacon, known locally as Wee Blinky, to reach the confluence of the Clyde and the White Cart.

► Turn left away from the Clyde and follow the quiet riverbank path along the Cart (the river begins its course several miles away high on Eaglesham Moor), home to heron and swans, passing the Normandy Hotel and a small boatyard to reach the historic St Conval and Argyll Stones. One of the

Ferry Tales The journey may only take a couple of minutes to complete, but the Renfrew to Yoker ferry service has provided a vital link for communities on both banks of the River Clyde for more than 200 years. Rowing boats initially provided transportation across the river, but by the 1930s a roll-on-roll-off car ferry was introduced. The building of the Clyde Tunnel and Erskine Bridge meant that by the 1970s the majority of ferries along the Clyde were not required. However, the Renfrew Ferry remained to transport shipyard workers across the Clyde, and in 2007 there were still over 150,000 passenger journeys annually.

stones was allegedly used by St Conval to cross the Irish Sea to Scotland where he founded a church near Renfrew in the 6th century, whilst the Argyll stone was apparently where the 9th Earl of Argyll was resting when he was arrested for treason in 1685 after leading an abortive Highland rebellion against James VII.

► The path branches here, so take the right fork to Inchinnan Road (A8) beside the distinct Inchinnan Bascule Bridge, a drawbridge (*bascule* is the French word for 'seesaw' and 'balance') that was built in 1923, allowing vessels to continue upstream to Paisley. Britain's best-known Bascule Bridge is Tower Bridge in London.

► Cross Inchinnan Road and go straight onto a cycletrack/walkway, signposted 'Porterfield Road', which continues along the White Cart. Again a lovely, quiet path makes its way beside the river (Babcock's, an engineering firm and important local employer, lies ahead – it has been based at this site since 1895), before bearing left away from the water to a fork. Take the right branch and follow this to reach Porterfield Road. Immediately, turn left onto Nethergreen Road and follow the pavement past houses and parkland. The road eventually veers right into Craigielea

Road, which is followed to the entrance gates of Robertson Park. The park opened in 1912 as a green space for the people of Renfrew and was gifted to the town by a successful local businessman, William Robertson.

▶ Turn left and make your way along a lovely beech-lined path through the park to return to Inchinnan Road

opposite two of Renfrew's finest buildings, the Police Station, opened in 1910, and the distinctive Victoria Baths, opened in 1921, after being gifted to the town by the fantastically named Lord and Lady Lobnitz, then owners of a local shipbuilding company.

▶ Turn right and follow the road back to the War Memorial.

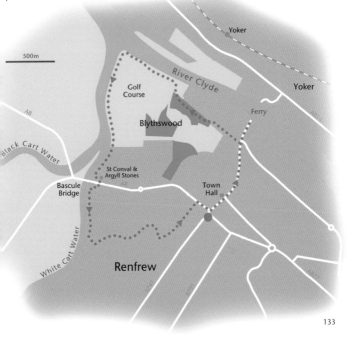

River Clyde at Renfrew

Erskine Bridge from the Kilpatrick Hills

# The Kilpatricks and the Forth & Clyde Canal

**Distance** 19km/12 miles
**Time** 6 hours
**Start/Finish** Kilpatrick Railway Station
GR NS468729
**Terrain** Minor roads, moorland paths
and tracks, cyclepath, canal towpath.
Some steep ascents and descents
and some sections of pathless terrain
**Map** OS Landranger 64
**Public transport** Regular Scotrail
trains from Glasgow Queen Street to
Old Kilpatrick

A combination of hill, moorland,
woodland and canal paths make up
this walk. It climbs high onto the
wild and wonderful Kilpatrick Hills,
where there are breathtaking views
along the River Clyde and towards
the Southern Highlands. The return
journey to Old Kilpatrick travels
along a section of the historic
Forth & Clyde Canal in the company
of a variety of wildlife.

► From Kilpatrick Railway Station,
climb Station Road to pass underneath
the railway line and then cross over
Mount Pleasant Drive. Once underneath
the A82, Station Road then swings
right. Leave it here, go straight on
and follow a minor road, which climbs
to a road on the right, signposted
'Loch Humphrey'.

► Walk up here, passing a couple of
cottages to join a rougher track which
continues to rise high above the
River Clyde. Some magnificent views
quickly open out along the Clyde towards
the industrial settings of Clydebank and
Greenock. Continue to climb the track
through a number of gates with the
gradient steepening until the track
passes above a steep gorge. The incline
now eases and it is a simple walk
through the increasingly untamed
landscape of the Kilpatrick Hills to reach
Loch Humphrey, home of Bearsden
Angling Club.

► The track continues beneath the
southern banks of the loch and crosses a
bridge over an outflow. It then swings
left away from Loch Humphrey and
narrows to a path. Follow this north over
boggier ground to begin a steeper climb
onto an obvious ridgeline. The path

**Saints and Sinners** Situated on the
north bank of the River Clyde, Old
Kilpatrick is named after St Patrick, the
patron saint of Ireland – there is a myth
that he was born here. Old Kilpatrick is
perhaps best known as the western
terminus of the Antonine Wall, the
northwest frontier of the Roman Empire,
which was built across Central Scotland
by the Romans between 142 and 144AD.

heads northeast along the ridge by Fynloch Hill, but then becomes a little sketchy as a craggier slope climbs onto an unnamed hill.

▶ The views towards Duncolm and of Ben Lomond, Stob Binnein and Ben More are stunning. Drop steeply northeast and then make the final steep pull on to Duncolm, which translates from Gaelic as the 'Fort of Columba'.

▶ Retrace your steps back to Loch Humphrey and once over the bridge climb the steep embankment to the lochside. Turn left and follow a path along the embankment which then drops down and continues to a gate beside a conifer plantation. Go through the gate onto a solid path, which travels above the remainder of Loch Humphrey. Once away from the water, the path continues through thicker woodland, in turn crossing a stone bridge and passing a lochan to reach a junction.

▶ Turn left where the woodland track begins a gradual descent following 'Crags Circular Path' signposts (these waymarks are followed all the way to Milton). At a fork, keep straight ahead and descend by Greenlands Reservoir with the track eventually passing through a gate and out of the woodland. After the next gate, beside a 'Crags' waymark, a fenced path (granting some fine views of Dumbarton Rock) drops down through a series of gates, and around three sides of a field to reach a minor road just west of Greenlands Farm. Turn right and walk down the road as it meanders through peaceful countryside. In due course, the road bears left onto Milton Brae and continues towards Milton.

▶ Just before entering Milton, turn right onto a narrow road (signed 'Crags Walk and Milton Inn 700m'). Just before a driveway, bear left onto a footpath. Walk along the waymarked path, crossing Colquhoun Drive to reach the A82 at the Milton Inn. Cross the A82 onto a path (signposted 'Crags Walk') to reach a cycletrack. Turn left (leaving the Crags Walk) and follow this beside the railway

**Vital Statistics** The Forth & Clyde Canal was constructed between 1768 and 1790, connecting the narrowest part of Scotland between the rivers of Forth and Clyde. The aim was to eliminate the long and risky journey around Scotland's coastline. The canal brought many trade opportunities for communities along its length, particularly at the natural inlet of Bowling Basin, the canal's western limit. The basin, with its dry dock and harbour, became a small hub for shipbuilding during the 18th and 19th centuries. Today, Bowling Basin is used as a mooring for a variety of pleasure craft.

line, for approximately 0.75 miles to the outskirts of Bowling. Cross the A814 onto another cycletrack and continue into Bowling, returning to the A814 at a set of traffic lights. Go straight across the road onto a minor road signposted 'Forth & Clyde Canal' and follow this down to the canal at Bowling Basin.

▶ Cross the canal by a bridge, turn left and follow the wonderful towpath along the canal (keeping an eye out for coot,

little grebe and tufted duck) for just over one mile. At Lock 37, just before passing underneath the Erskine Bridge, turn left and cross back over the canal by the lock to reach the A814 (Dumbarton Road). Turn left to walk through Old Kilpatrick, turning right onto Station Road.

Duncolm Hill

Dumbarton Castle

# Dumbarton and Dumbarton Rock

**Distance** 8km/5 miles
**Time** 2 hours
**Start/Finish** Dumbarton Central Station GR NS397755
**Terrain** Pavement, riverside and parkland paths
**Map** OS Landranger 63/64
**Public transport** Regular trains between Glasgow Central and Dumbarton Central railway stations

The River Clyde and the River Leven bound Dumbarton on its southern and western limits. Like many towns along the Clyde, heavy industry has been central to Dumbarton's development, and this absorbing walk passes many fine buildings linked to its industrial past. In sharp contrast the route also travels through the peaceful Levengrove Park. No walk around Dumbarton would be complete without a visit to the craggy Dumbarton Rock and its resplendent castle.

▶ From Dumbarton Central go through a gate at the corner of Station Road and Church Street into the grounds of the Municipal Buildings. Walk along a path, turning right through one of the archways of St Mary's Collegiate Church of Dumbarton, founded in 1453. Continue around the

front of the Municipal Building, passing the statue of Peter Denny who, along with his brothers William and Alexander, founded the world-famous Denny shipbuilders in 1842 – over the next 121 years the company built, amongst others, *The Cutty Sark*. Exit right onto College Street and then left back onto Station Road. Follow Station Road to a set of traffic lights on Glasgow Road

**Briton's Got Talent** A volcanic plug of rock has shaped Dumbarton's history. Dumbarton Rock was a strategically important settlement as far back as the Iron Age, and strong trading links were forged as a result. Fragments of Roman pottery, German glassware and Mediterranean ceramics have all been excavated within the town.

Until the end of the Middle Ages, Dumbarton was a major British political centre. It was the capital of the ancient Kingdom of Strathclyde until 1018, illustrated by the Gaelic translation of the name Dumbarton as 'Fort of the Britons'.

The settlement was sacked in 870AD by Vikings and it struggled to retain its status as a commercial hub. Nevertheless, Dumbarton was granted Royal Burgh status in 1222, with Dumbarton Castle becoming a Royal Castle. By the early 17th century it had become a major port again.

(A814) beside Dumbarton Health Centre, which used to be the site of Dumbarton Gasworks.

► Cross Glasgow Road onto High Street, then turn right onto Bridge Street. Cross the impressive Dumbarton Bridge over the River Leven, enjoying some marvellous views of Ben Lomond. Once over the bridge, immediately turn left onto Woodyard Road and walk along the pavement, bearing right at Levenford Terrace into Levengrove Park.

Rock of Ages The volcanic plug of Dumbarton Rock dominates the town. Sitting on its steep slopes is Dumbarton Castle, built by Alexander II of Scotland in 1220 as a defensive fortification in response to the threat from Norway, whose kings ruled the Hebrides and the islands in the Clyde. There is evidence of a settlement here from around 450AD when it was known as *Alt Clut*, the 'Fort of the Clyde'. The castle's political importance declined over subsequent centuries, although Mary Queen of Scots was secretly sheltered here as a five year old before being taken to France during the 'Rough Wooing'.

During the Second World War, Dumbarton was heavily bombed by the German Luftwaffe as it targeted the important shipyards of the Clyde.

► A path climbs through the parkland, going straight on at a crossroads. Keep on through the park as the path swings left by the ruins of the old St Serf's Church of Cardross. At a junction, turn right and follow the tree-lined path, bearing left onto a path just before a war memorial to reach the Clyde. Walk along an indistinct grassy path above the river, with exceptional views of Dumbarton Rock ahead. The path becomes more obvious and soon veers left to a minor road. Go straight across, past a football pitch and back to the River Leven.

► Turn left, walk, following the river back onto Woodyard Road and turn right back over Dumbarton Bridge. Once across, immediately turn right down a flight of steps signposted 'Riverside Walk' and follow the path, which culminates beside the old red sandstone Inverleven Distillery.

► Turn left onto Riverside Lane and then right onto High Street. This pavement leads you onto Castle Street, which reaches Glasgow Road beside the excellent Scottish Maritime Museum. Turn right, continue through Dumbarton, turning right again onto Victoria Road, signposted 'Dumbarton Castle'. With the magnificent profile of Dumbarton Rock ahead follow Victoria Road onto Castle Road, pass by Dumbarton Football Club, formed in

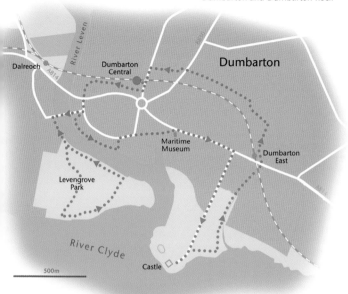

1872, and the Rock Bowling Club – surely one of the most picturesque greens in Britain – to arrive at Dumbarton Rock and the castle.

▶ Retrace your steps a short way from the castle, then turn right onto a path signposted 'Castle Circular Path'. Go through a gate to take a path which journeys above the Clyde and then swings left to travel alongside a burn. Cross a footbridge and then go left at a fork. Continue to a barrier, go around this and turn left onto a single-track road to reach Castlegreen Street. Go straight across onto a path, which runs parallel with the burn and Buchanan Street, passing under a railway bridge.

▶ Cross Glasgow Road into East End Park, where a path leads you left to a junction. Turn right, then left at the next junction and continue to reach Crosslet Road. Turn left, follow the pavement by Dumbarton Academy, turning left onto Bonhill Road, then right onto Bankend Road. Walk along the pavement and at Church Street turn left, pass under a railway bridge and then right onto Station Road to return to the start.

Dumbarton Rock

Bust of John Logie Baird

# Helensburgh and Rhu

Distance **8.5km/5.25 miles**
Time **2 hours 30**
Start/Finish **Helensburgh Pier
GR NS295822**
Terrain **Pavement, woodland paths,
single-track road, promenade**
Map **OS Landranger 56**
Public transport **Regular trains from
Glasgow Queen Street and
Edinburgh Waverley to Helensburgh**

The coastal town of Helensburgh on
the banks of the Firth of Clyde is an
attractive setting for the River Clyde
to reach its journey's end. From the
mid-19th century, Helensburgh
became a popular destination for
holidaymakers to enjoy the spa baths
and clean sea air. This bracing walk
sets out from Helensburgh Pier to
climb steeply through the town, past
the iconic Mackintosh-designed Hill
House and into beautiful woodland
high above Helensburgh with
dazzling views of the coast. The tree-
lined paths drop down into the
village of Rhu, from where an easy
stroll above the Firth of Clyde leads
back to Helensburgh.

▶ From Helensburgh Pier, at the corner
of Clyde Street (A814) and Sinclair Street
(A818), follow Sinclair Street as it climbs
steeply through the town, passing St
Andrews Kirk, Victoria Halls and
Helensburgh Upper Railway Station.

After one mile, turn left onto Kennedy
Drive (signposted 'Hill House'), then
right onto Upper Colquhoun Street to
climb up to Hill House.

▶ Walk by Hill House and through the
car park to reach a path signposted for
Rhu Marina. Turn left through a gate to
enter a strip of beautiful oak and birch
woodland. From here, the path travels

## Planning for the Holidays

Helensburgh was named in honour of
Lady Helen Sutherland, wife of Sir James
Colquhoun of Luss, who bought the
land in and around the fishing village of
Millig in 1752 – the name Millig can still
be seen in various forms around town.
Helensburgh was developed in 1776,
and was planned as a grid street system.

In 1808, Henry Bell, an engineer,
bought the public baths, as well as the
hotel which his wife ran. To boost his
trade, Bell commissioned John & Charles
Wood, Port Glasgow shipbuilders, to
build a paddle steamer to bring
potential customers from Glasgow to the
hotel in Helensburgh. *The Comet*,
Europe's first commercial steamboat,
embarked upon its maiden voyage from
Glasgow's Broomielaw to Helensburgh
in August 1812.

In the 1850s, the arrival of the
Glasgow to Helensburgh railway link
increased Helensburgh's popularity as
an accessible seaside resort.

northwest over several footbridges where you may spot woodpecker, whinchat and redwing. Bluebell, wood anemone and wild garlic flourish on the woodland floor during spring and summer. The solid path leads high above Helensburgh to a gate, offering fine views across the Firth of Clyde. Once through the gate, bear left to cross a bridge over a burn. The path then swings right over another bridge and by a signpost for Rhu Marina.

▶ Three more bridges are crossed with the path culminating at the Highlandman's Road, an ancient Right of Way used until the 19th century by those living in Glen Fruin wishing to attend church in Rhu.

House on the Hill Glasgow School of Art may be Charles Rennie Mackintosh's greatest work, but many people consider Hill House a close second. In 1902 Walter Blackie, a successful Glasgow publisher, commissioned Mackintosh and his wife Margaret MacDonald to design a lavish family home. The final design was strongly influenced by the Art Nouveau Glasgow style that Mackintosh and MacDonald were celebrated for, and Hill House was completed in 1903. It passed into the care of the National Trust for Scotland in 1982 and remains one of Helensburgh's most popular attractions.

▶ Turn left onto the broad track of the Highlandman's Road, which climbs gently through Highlandman's Wood, the trees thinning at points to give fleeting glimpses of the Clyde. It eventually drops quite steeply through a gate from which point the track descends gradually alongside an open field, where livestock may be grazing. After passing through two gates in quick succession, a minor road then drops down towards Rhu, passing Torrs Farm, and over a railway bridge onto Station Road. At a mini roundabout bear left onto Pier Road and continue a short distance to reach a rougher road on the right. Follow this down to reach the A814 at Rhu.

▶ Cross the road onto a pavement and turn left. Follow this above Gare Loch, enjoying some great views across to the Rosneath Peninsula, and pass Rhu Marina. The pavement continues easily back into Helensburgh and onto the seafront promenade. This is a lovely stretch of walkway, which travels above the Firth of Clyde and past the bust of John Logie Baird and the monument to Henry Bell to reach Helensburgh Pier.

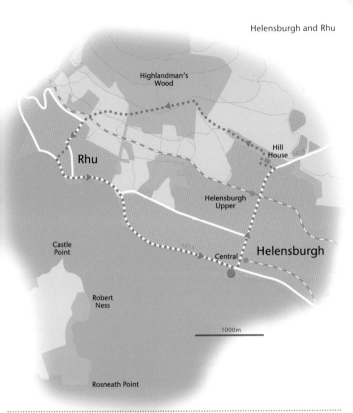

**Helensburgh Hero** Pioneer of television and radio, John Logie Baird was a son of the manse born in Helensburgh in 1888. He studied at Glasgow's Royal Technical College (now the University of Strathclyde) before emigrating to Trinidad to run a jam factory. On his return in 1923 he moved to Hastings on the south coast of England where he began experimenting, using crude apparatus, with the concept of television. By 1926 Baird had managed to transmit a flickering image from one room to another. He continued to work on a television service but was left behind by a similar innovation by Marconi-EMI. Baird died in Bexhill-on-Sea in 1946, and was buried in Helensburgh Cemetery.

Helensburgh seafront

The Arrochar Alp from Greenock Cut

# Greenock Cut

**Distance** 10.5km/6.5 miles
**Time** 2 hours 30
**Start/Finish** Parking at Greenock Cut
Visitor Centre GR NS247721
**Terrain** Pavement, single-track road,
woodland paths
**Map** OS Landranger 63
**Public transport** None to start

The Greenock Cut aqueduct was
built in 1825 to supply the residents
and mills of Greenock with fresh
water from Loch Thom. The wide-
open spaces and clean air of the
Cut are in marked contrast to the
industrial heritage of Greenock
below. A tunnel now carries water
to Greenock, but the legacy of
Greenock Cut (now an Ancient
Monument and a central feature of
Clyde Muirshiel Park) is a superb
6.5-mile circular walk. It passes 23
beautiful stone bridges, and two
bothies that provided basic
accommodation for the workers
when the Cut was being built. Add
to this the wonderful wildlife and
some of the best views in Southern
Scotland (the Cowal Peninsula, the
River Clyde, Arran and the Arrochar
Alps are all clearly visible) and you
have a great walk.

► From Greenock Cut Visitor Centre car
park, turn right onto a single-track road
where the road immediately splits. Take

the centre path, which leads down to a
gate. Go through this, turn left over a
bridge and then turn right onto a path,
following this by a waterfall through
some wonderfully peaceful countryside.
The path then goes through another
gate and here it forks. Take the right fork
and follow the path past Shielhall Farm.
Beyond a gate, cross a single-track road,
and go through another gate.

► An excellent path continues high
above the River Clyde, passing superb
old stone bridges and some of the
workers' huts that were built during the
construction of Greenock Cut. Eventually
the path passes through another gate
where the views across the Firth of
Clyde towards Arran, as well as those of

**Parklife** Covering 108 square miles,
Clyde Muirshiel Park is Scotland's largest
regional park, a status it has enjoyed
since it was formally designated in 1990.
It includes Lochwinnoch, Castle Semple
Loch, Lunderston Bay and Greenock Cut
and covers sections of Inverclyde,
Renfrewshire and Ayrshire – there are
fine views across these regions. The
diverse landscape means an abundance
of wildlife can be found around Clyde
Muirshiel, including roe deer, lapwing,
snipe, oystercatcher, curlew, swans,
buzzard, sparrowhawk, hen harrier,
meadow pipit, common hawker
dragonfly and green hairstreak butterfly.

the Arrochar Alps, the Luss Hills and the Cowal Peninsula, are stunning. Follow the path as it snakes its way across the countryside and through another gate high above the town of Greenock. It then veers right above a steep gorge, crosses a bridge beside a waterfall and sweeps left to continue above the gorge.

▶ Once across another stone bridge, a grassy path cuts through some woodland and another gate. After crossing a footbridge over a burn, the path meanders alongside birch, rowan and hawthorn trees towards Overton, and there are further great views down onto Greenock with the shipbuilding cranes particularly prominent.

▶ Go through a gate, cross another bridge and then pass through two more gates to approach a cottage at Overton. Just before the cottage turn right, cross a bridge and go through a gate onto a broad track, which climbs gently away from Overton. Passing a small reservoir, the views over the River Clyde to Helensburgh, the Cowal Peninsula and the broad sweep of the Southern Highlands are breathtaking. On reaching a fork, take the right track, which passes another reservoir, and go through a gate.

▶ Follow the track as it climbs steadily by the wonderfully named Scroggy Bank to a fork. Take the left branch, where the track drops gently past Loch Thom, a lovely, tranquil spot, the loch itself providing a great point to view the wilder aspects of Clyde Muirshiel Park.

▶ At Loch Thom Cottage, go through a gate onto a single-track road and follow this by Compensation Reservoir back towards Greenock Cut Visitor Centre. The road passes a café and through one final gate to reach the visitor centre.

Shipyards and Sugar Greenock takes its name from the Gaelic *Grianaig*, meaning the 'Sunny Hillock'. It is sometimes, incorrectly, said that it derived from 'Green Oak' – a green oak is used in the logo for the town's main shopping centre, the Oak Mall.
   By the early 1600s a pier had been built on the Clyde here and Greenock was quickly established as a port. After the 1707 Act of Union it became the main port for the West Indies and one of the Clyde's most famous yards, Scotts, was established in 1711 (ships were built here for an incredible 277 years). As well as shipbuilding, sugar refining played a prominent role in Greenock's prosperity during the 1800s, with 14 refineries processing sugar from the Caribbean. The prosperity of that time is still reflected in some of Greenock's outstanding buildings including Custom House and Victoria Tower.

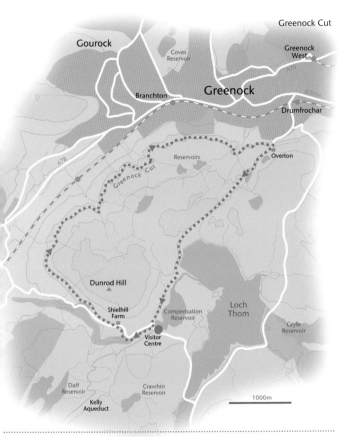

Water Course Designed by the Ayrshire-born engineer Robert Thom and built between 1825 and 1827, the Greenock Cut aqueduct carried water from Compensation Reservoir below Loch Thom down to Greenock just over two miles away. The Cut fed two mill lades which descended through the town to empty into the Clyde and companies rented individual falls from these to power their machinery. Among the enterprises which relied on the Cut at its peak were flour, paper, flax and woollen mills, rope-works, foundries and sugar refineries.

Greenock from Greenock Cut

# Index